ADVENTURES
IN GRILLING

COOKING WITH FIRE AND SMOKE

RECIPES
WILLIE COOPER

DRINK RECIPES
JORDAN MACKAY

TEXT
FRED THOMPSON

PHOTOGRAPHY
RAY KACHATORIAN

*weldon*owen

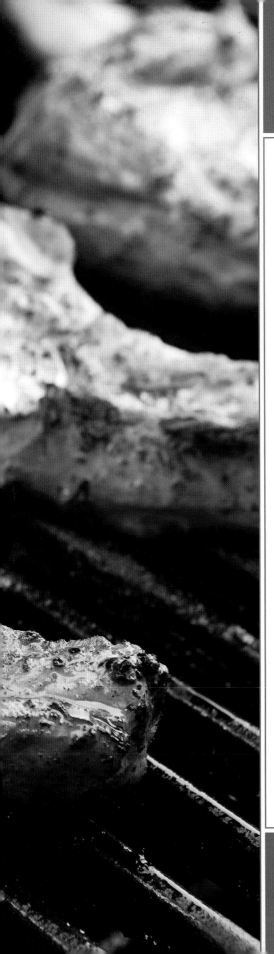

Contents

Grilling Equipment

There is a grill for every situation. Sure, we all think of full-sized grills when visions of a sizzling steak or sauce-slathered ribs drift through our minds, but small grills for a quick trip to the beach or a balcony also yield great smoking flavor.

Charcoal Grills

Charcoal grills come in almost any size or shape. Sizes range from small portable grills to popular 22-inch (51-cm)-round kettle grills to even larger rectangular grills. Look for stability, good-quality construction, and adjustable vents and a lid that allow you to control your fire. If you plan to smoke foods, a side firebox is handy. A standard-sized kettle grill fits the needs of most grillers. In any case, a sturdy, high-quality grill will last longest and be most economical over time.

Gas Grills

Gas grills range from simple to fully-loaded models with smoke boxes, rotisserie and side burners, and infrared searing sections. Two burners are necessary if you plan to cook with indirect heat, but a three-burner unit will give you more heat control and is the best choice for many. Don't get carried away with BTUs; 35,000 is fine for most of us. Look at how the heat is dispersed. Angled metal plates that cover each burner deliver more even heat with fewer flare-ups; stainless steel or powder paint–coated stainless grill racks conduct heat well. Infrared technology is more apparent in gas grills today; they cook slightly differently.

Grill Pans

Don't let the weather or apartment-house rules keep you from achieving grilled flavor. Grill pans can rescue you; they cover one or two cooking elements on your range. Cast iron is ideal for a grill pan, as it provides a good sear and with the pre-seasoned models, it's also easy to use.

Portable Grills

There is no reason not to take grilling on the road. Many grocery stores stock disposable aluminum grills in their picnic sections, especially during the summer. Small, reusable bucket grills are also handy, some are even gas powered by small propane tanks. Look for grills whose frames and legs fold easily for transport.

TAKING CARE OF YOUR GRILL

Grills are generally low maintenance, but they still need to be cared for. Here are a few simple rules to ensure that your grill cooks efficiently for many years to come:

• Read the owner's manual that comes with the grill before cooking on it for the first time. Be sure to note cleaning instructions.

• Brush the grill grate with oil before you begin to cook. This will prevent food from sticking and will make cleanup easier.

• After you have finished grilling, when the grill is still hot, use a wire brush to remove any food that is stuck to the grill grate.

• Don't let ashes accumulate in a charcoal grill. Wait until the ash is cold, scoop it out, and discard in a heatproof container.

• When your gas grill has completely cooled, clean gas jets by scraping off accumulated grease with a metal scraper.

• Protect your grill with a waterproof cover or store it indoors.

Grilling Accessories

Gadgets abound in the grilling world. Some are essential, such as an instant-read thermometer. Others are fun to have and useful, like rib racks, a clip-on light, and beer-can chicken racks. Here's the skinny on what you really need.

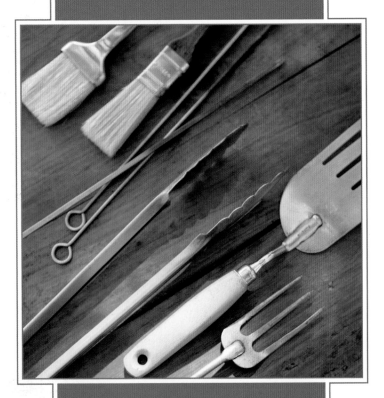

Thermometers

A good instant-read thermometer is indispensable. Simply insert the thermometer into your protein towards the end of the cooking time; the temperature will register in seconds. Never let it touch any bone, which will give you a false reading, and don't leave it in the meat while cooking. Calibrate your thermometer every now and then, according to the manufacturer's instructions.

Skewers

Metal or wood: The great skewer debate rages on. If you grill lots of skewered foods, get a set of flat-sided metal skewers, at least 8 inches (20 cm) long. The metal conducts heat, which will insure proper cooking. If using wooden skewers, soak them first in water—or, for extra flavor, beer, wine, or juice—for 30 minutes.

Grill Baskets, Screens, and Plates

Grill baskets are good for delicate foods that are difficult to turn or that could fall through the cooking grate, such as asparagus, fish fillets, and onions. Screens and plates have similar uses. A screen is like a wire mesh supported by a metal frame; a plate is a sheet of metal that is perforated with small holes and helps prevent flare-ups. Place each of them over direct heat, brush with oil, and let them heat for a minute or two to minimize sticking.

Tools

A long-handled wire brush designed solely for cleaning grills is a must. The bristles should be rustproof. Use the brush when the grill is hot, both before and after cooking your food. A stainless steel scraper with a wooden or heatproof plastic or silicone handle is good for cleaning in-between the grill grates. A set of long-handled tongs is the best for turning most grilled foods. Silicone brushes make coating your foods with sauces a breeze and are easy to clean. For foods that need to be flipped, you'll need a spatula. Get one with a medium-length handle, which will give you more control. Make sure that the handle has some insulation.

Smoker Boxes

Smoker boxes are heavy, vented metal containers that hold wood chips or herbs to create a flavoring smoke on a gas grill. After the wood chips are soaked for 30 minutes, add them to the smoker box and place it directly over a gas burner. Preheat your grill as usual; smoke should be present when you start to cook. Reduce the burner under the box to low heat, but don't shut it off. Smoke from a smoke box will last about 20 minutes. You can also fashion a smoke box out of heavy-duty foil. Take a 12-by-18-inch (30-by-45 cm) piece and add wood chips or herbs in the center. Close the packet and punch several holes in the foil to allow smoke to escape. Then proceed as with the smoke box.

Chimney Starters

Chimney charcoal starters are a safe, relatively environmentally friendly, and efficient way to light a charcoal fire. Plus, you have the added benefit of no lighter-fluid aftertaste in your food. Chimney starters are tall cylinders made of metal with vents at the bottom, a rack inside, and a handle on one side. They range in size, so buy one to fit the amount of charcoal your grill needs. A chimney 7.5 inches (19 cm) in diameter and 12 inches (30 cm) tall will fit the bill for most medium to large kettle grills. If in doubt, buy the larger size. For instructions on use, see page 15.

Rotisserie Attachment

A rotisserie consists of a large spit that is powered by an electric motor. It slowly rotates at a constant speed above the fire bed, making it a good choice for grilling a large roast or whole bird. When choosing a rotisserie, look for a model with a strong, reliable motor and a sturdy counterweight system.

Protective Gear

Have on hand an oven mitt and a pot holder made of heavy quilted cotton to protect your hands from intense heat. Leather grill gloves also help prevent burns.

Fueling the Fire

Today's griller has many choices when it comes to fueling the grill. Knowing about the different types of fuel—charcoal, wood chunks, or propane—will help you make the best selection for your grill. Be sure to also read the owner's manual for specific fuels best suited for your type of grill.

Charcoal

For decades, most charcoal grillers have used briquettes. They burn for a long time and generate consistent heat, making them a very good choice for indirect-heat cooking. Avoid brands with nitrates, petroleum, sand, or clay, and avoid self-starting charcoal altogether. Natural hardwood charcoal gives you a subtle smoke flavor as you cook. It burns much hotter than briquettes and has a tendency to spark. Hardwood is perfect for quick direct-heat cooking and for indirect-heat cooking as well. This is the preferred charcoal of most championship pitmasters and serious grillers everywhere. Pay close attention the first few times you use hardwood charcoal; it cooks differently. With either type, you may need a little trial and error to hone your techniques, as the temperature of charcoal is more difficult to control than gas. Store both briquettes and charcoal in a cool, dry place.

Wood Chips and Chunks

Wood adds more flavor to food than any other grilling fuel. Bags of chips as well as large chunks of hickory, apple, and mesquite are readily available today. Wood is also cantankerous and a difficult fuel to work with when used alone. Many factors affect how wood chips and chunks burn, but the moisture content is the most crucial. If they are bone dry, wood chips and chunks will go up in smoke before the food has a chance to pick up much smokiness. But soaking them in water or a flavorful liquid before adding them to the fire ensures that they will burn slowly and evenly, creating a steady flow of smoke that will permeate every inch of the food being cooked.

Propane

If you have a gas grill, don't let the charcoal folks bully you. Propane is efficient, environmentally friendly, and cost effective. Repeated taste tests continue to show that with most grilled foods, charcoal and gas rank about the same in flavor. Always check for gas leaks when you change propane tanks; your manufacturer's manual will tell you how for your model. While a propane tank lasts a long time, always have a spare in case it runs out. Store tanks outside, but not in direct sunlight and away from heat. When trading tanks, reject any that appear rusted, even under fresh paint. The two drawbacks of propane are the missing smoke flavor and that its maximum temperature is less than lump charcoal. Both issues are easily addressed: Wood chips, which are easy to use, can add smoke flavor, and foods can simply be grilled longer on gas to achieve the same browning or doneness. Instead of propane, you can also go with a more permanent solution of natural gas, but be aware that most gas grills have to be adapted for natural gas, and that is best left to a professional. Going with natural gas also means your grill will no longer be portable.

FLAVORING YOUR FIRE

Besides the natural flavors that develop on the grill as proteins caramelize and juice drippings interact with the fire, you can add many other nuances. Wood chips or chunks, grapevines, and dried herbs contribute distinctive notes. Here's a quick guide: **Hickory, oak, mesquite,** and **pecan** are intense, with a woody flavor profile, and are good with pork, chicken, turkey, and beef. **Hickory** by itself is very strong, so temper it with another wood to balance flavor. **Fruit woods** like **apple, cherry, and plum**, are moderately intense and leave a sweetness. Try these—the current darlings of barbecue contests—with pork, salmon, game birds, and chicken, or anything with a sweet sauce. **Alderwood** is mild and perfect for fish. Leave soft woods like pine for the building industry. They taste terrible and the resin from pine and other soft woods could damage your grill. **Rosemary** cuttings and lamb are prefect for each other, and most any combination of herbs will deliver a subtle flavor to most any food.

Grilling Methods

Today's grills, gas and charcoal, are much more versatile than the braziers of the fifties and hibachis of the sixties. No matter what type of grill you have, it's important to understand direct- and indirect-heat cooking. With these two methods, all things are possible.

Direct Heat

When you need intense high heat to sear that steak or cook any item that will take less than 25 minutes, turn to direct-heat grilling. Simply put, direct-heat grilling occurs when you place food directly over hot coals or a preheated burner on a gas grill. This method gives food a nice sear, creating a flavorful caramelized crust. Direct-heat grilling can be done with or without a lid, but using a lid will reduce flare-ups and give you more even heat. The exception is tuna, which cooks too quickly covered. Direct-heat foods are usually seasoned with herbs and spices, but if you do plan to baste with a sugar-based sauce, do it at the end of the cooking time so it doesn't burn. Foods that take well to direct heat include steaks, chops, burgers, fish fillets, boneless chicken, sausages, and most vegetables.

Indirect Heat

Indirect-heat grilling involves placing the food away from the heat source. On a charcoal grill, that means pushing the charcoal to one side or both sides, leaving the center space without direct heat. With gas, preheat with all burners on, and then cut off one or more. Indirect-heat grilling is similar to roasting in the oven; heat is reflected and circulated around the food and it cooks slowly. Use indirect-heat grilling for foods that take more than 25 minutes. This is also the method that you use for smoking and barbecuing. The lid is always down with this no-fuss method. For long-cooking items on charcoal, check your coals after an hour to make sure you still have heat. And don't peek too much—you lose heat each time you lift the lid.

Hybrid

Hybrid grilling is using direct and indirect heat in concert when cooking foods that benefit from a good sear, but will take longer than 25 minutes to cook. This is an underused method and one that you should add to your grill master skills.

BUILDING A FIRE PIT

Chances are someone in your neighborhood has one—a fire pit. It's a modern way of sitting by the campfire. A fire pit is a sublime way to socialize and extend the summer patio season a few more months into the fall, or get an early jump on spring.

To build the pit: Choose a spot (be sure there are no underground cables or pipes in your location) and, if possible, clear an area of about 10 feet (3 m). On a nonflammable surface such as brick, gravel, or dirt, or in a metal fire ring, line the bottom and sides with large stones to retain the heat. Arrange hardwood logs or charcoal and kindling such as twigs or dried grass in a pyramid shape in the pit. Using a long match or lighter, ignite the hardwood logs and charcoal, and let them burn down 1–2 hours, until the embers are covered in ash. Continue to add wood and charcoal to maintain a constant temperature throughout the cooking process.

Starting the Charcoal Grill

A chimney starter (see page 9) is far superior to any other method of lighting charcoal. To use a chimney starter, lightly stuff newspaper in the bottom with the vents. Using too much paper will actually smother the fire; usually, 2 sheets will work. Next, pour charcoal briquettes or hardwood charcoal into the top of the chimney, filling it completely. Light the paper using a fireplace match or gas wand. The fire will burn upward and ignite the charcoal. Let the coals burn until they are ash gray in color, 15 to 20 minutes. Lift the chimney starter by the handle (use an oven mitt) and carefully pour the coals on the fire grate in your grill. This method is effective and more environmentally friendly, and leaves none of the aftertaste that can come from petroleum-based charcoal starters.

Indirect and Direct Heat

To set up an indirect-heat fire in a charcoal grill, use long-handled tongs to push the hot coals to either side of the grill. Place a drip pan in the center, where there are no coals. Put the food on the center of the grill rack directly over the pan and cover the grill. For direct-heat cooking, use long-handled tongs to spread the hot coals evenly across the fire bed directly below where the food will cook.

Firing Up a Charcoal Grill

Starting and maintaining the fire in any type of grill should be a stress free experience. Using a chimney starter is the way to go for charcoal. Once those coals are lit, you'll also need to arrange them into the perfect fire bed. Here's how.

CHECKING FOR DONENESS

The immense number of variables that factor into the art of grilling sometimes make it difficult to determine whether that item on the grill is done. When following any recipe, use cooking times as a guide rather than exact indicators. Weather conditions, the temperature of the food before you started grilling, and its size and thickness can all vary from recipe to reality. Internal temperature is the best and most accurate gauge of doneness, so count on an instant-read thermometer to be your best teacher in the learning curve. Also keep in mind that food always continues to cook after it's been removed from the grill.

The pros use touch as a guide, and there are a couple of methods. Here's a quick version: With your mouth slightly open, push on your cheek. That's close to what rare meat feels like when prodded. Push the point of your nose for medium, and your forehead for well done. As you check your foods, use these points and a thermometer, and pretty soon you'll be a pro at estimating doneness.

Firing Up a Gas Grill

Starting a gas grill seems simple compared to a charcoal grill, yet it too has its demands. Read your owner's manual and get familiar with the components of the grill. The manual will also tell you how to check for gas leaks.

Starting the Gas Grill

Open the lid on your grill. Turn on the valve on the propane tank, all the way to open. With natural gas, open the valve. Turn all of your burners to high and then push the igniter button. If you don't have an automatic igniter, use a long match or gas wand to light the burners. Close the lid and allow the temperature to rise to at least 350°F (180°C), higher is better for steaks, burgers, and chops. With most gas grills, this will take about 15 minutes. When ready to cook, open the lid and adjust the burner controls to the heat level that works best for your food.

Indirect and Direct Heat

For an indirect-heat fire in a gas grill, preheat the grill using all the burners, and then turn off the burners that are directly beneath where the food will sit and place a drip pan below the grate. For direct-heat fire, heat all burners beneath the grate.

For precise heat measurement, use a thermometer to gauge the temperature. To do the hand test, hold your hand about 4 inches (10 cm) above the fire. Keep your hand there as long as you can and count; refer to the chart for the approximate temperature.

CHARCOAL GRILL TEMPERATURE CHART

Heat level	Appearance of coals	Hand test
Very high	Glowing brightly	less than 1 second
High	Glowing brightly	1 or 2 seconds
Medium-high	Glowing brightly; faint coating of ash	2 or 3 seconds
Medium	Glowing; light coating of ash	3 or 4 seconds
Medium-low	Faint glow; moderate coating of ash	3 or 4 seconds
Low	Barely glowing; thick coating of ash	5 seconds or more

GAS GRILL TEMPERATURE CHART

Heat level	Temperature	Hand test
Very high	450°F (230°C) and higher	less than 1 second
High	400°–450°F (200°–230°C)	1 or 2 seconds
Medium-high	375°–400°F (190°–200°C)	2 or 3 seconds
Medium	350°–375°F (180°–190°C)	3 or 4 seconds
Medium-low	300°–350°F (150°–180°C)	3 or 4 seconds
Low	200°–300°F (95°–150°C)	5 seconds or more

Grilling Guidelines

Tips for Successful Grilling

Cooking with fire is fun but can be a dangerous sport. As with mastering any skill, learning to grill means starting with the basics. Just like playing piano or football, there's some simple guidelines to follow. Here are 20 rules of thumb to keep in mind when firing up the coals.

1 Be patient and let your grill fully preheat; make sure your charcoal is ash-gray before you begin grilling.

2 Keep your cooking grate clean.

3 Oil the cooking grate each time you cook and brush or spray oil on your food, especially fish; sticking will become a thing of the past. Oil also transfers heat quickly.

4 Understand direct- and indirect-heat cooking and when to use each or a combination.

5 Never leave your grill unattended.

6 Shoot for caramelization, not blackening.

7 Don't baste with sauces that include sugar until the end of the cooking time. That includes ketchup-based sauces.

8 Turn food only once, if at all possible.

9 Use a thermometer to gauge both grill temperature and internal food temperature (at least until you have mastered the "touch" method for doneness; see page 15).

10 Check for gas leaks every time you change a propane tank. It's very simple to do with a spray bottle filled with soapy water; if there is a leak, bubbles will appear.

11 Don't wear loose clothes while grilling.

12 When grilling outside, keep the grill away from overhangs.

13 Never light a gas grill with the lid closed.

14 Watch the kids when the grill is in use.

15 Don't try to move a lit grill.

16 If a gas grill's burner doesn't light, shut everything off, including the tank, open the lid, and wait at least 5 minutes before trying again. If it continues, check your owner's manual for how to clear a blockage.

17 Follow the owner's manual for recommendations on scheduled maintenance on your grill. It will make your life easier and extend the life of your investment.

18 With a gas grill, if you smell gas, there's a problem. Shut everything down. If you still continue to smell gas, call your friendly fire department.

19 Always shut the vents and place the lid on a charcoal grill to smother the fire. Make sure the ashes are completely cold before disposing of them.

20 Most of all enjoy the process, and reap the rewards, and praise.

FLARE-UPS

A flare-up is likely to occur sometime in your grilling career, so the best thing you can do is to plan for it. This happens when fat drips onto the heat source and causes flames to flare during grilling. When the situation arises, the first step is to not panic. The second step is to move the food to the open space or cooler part of the grill and, if needed, cover the grill and close its vents. A good preventative measure is to never leave the grill unattended—flare-ups tend to occur most when food is not being watched, resulting in lots of flames and charred food. Once you have cleared the danger zone, let the fat burn until it's completely gone. Some cooks control the flames by dousing them with water from a spray bottle. This should be a last resort, because the steam from flames sprayed too close to you can cause burns; plus, cold water can crack the finish of a hot grill. After you've battled a flare-up, be sure to clean out all of the burnt grease and food from the bottom of the grill after it's cold.

Meat

When selecting beef, seek out bright red meat with light marbling, a fine texture, and nearly white outer fat. The exterior fat should be minimal. Choose pork that is well trimmed with no dark patches or blemishes; avoid any that looks watery or has a gray cast to it. Look for meat that is hormone free and purchase from a reputable butcher or grocery store.

Poultry

Poultry should have even coloring, from white to pale yellow to ivory. Look for plump birds with well-defined breasts and legs. Any visible fat should be white to light yellow, and the skin should be unbroken and clean and appear dry. Look for hormone-free birds that are raised free range and fed organic grain.

Fish

Always buy fish fresh from a reputable fishmonger and cook it the day you buy it. It should look moist and bright and should have a fresh scent. Shrimp should be purchased in the shell and should not have yellowing or black-spotted shells. Oysters and mussels should be closed tightly and feel heavy with water.

Fruits & Vegetables

The most important advice when buying fruits and vegetables is to buy locally and follow the seasons. The freshest produce that you can find will yield the most flavorful results.

Flavorings

The many flavors in this book range from fresh garden herbs to hoppy beer from the fridge. When it comes to salt, sea salt adds lots of flavor, and the chunky grains of coarse salt tend to go well with meat. Pepper should be freshly ground or cracked. Granulated garlic is used in many recipes in this book; don't substitute garlic powder for it. Agave syrup, a liquid sweetener, is also used frequently; it can be replaced with honey.

Choosing Ingredients

Knowing your ingredients will make your grilling experiences more satisfying and better tasting. Focus on buying the best ingredients you can and using the proper charcoal or gas grilling method to cook them.

Beer Pairing Guide

Grilled Foods and Beer

A cold beer is usually somewhere close by any grill. Any beer makes for a good match with grilled foods. As appreciation for pairing foods with wine has grown, so has interest in beers of different styles and characteristics. Many of the best matches with roasted and grilled foods share that "roasty" quality. Pork cracklings, crispy chicken skin, and grilled onions all have a sweet quality, and they go beautifully with beers that also have a nice, malty sweetness.

BEEF

Try a **porter** with beef. Porters are dark and rich, but without the malt flavor of a stout. The beer is probably named for the porters who carried goods around 19th-century London. Guess where they drank? Porterhouses. And what cut of beef did they prefer? Porterhouse steaks. A full-bodied ale, such as **India Pale Ale (IPA)**, also fares well with grilled burgers or steak.

PORK

Belgian bière de garde, a "farmhouse" ale, has spicy, peppery, and herbal notes that blend with pork that is not covered with barbecue sauce. A good, sturdy **stout** or a nice malty, sweet German wheat beer such as **hefeweizen** also stands up well next to a grilled pork tenderloin or chop.

LAMB

German **schwarzbier** is the darkest of the lagers and offers a good balance to the fattiness of lamb. A **Marzen**, a pale but strong lager, can also be served.

POULTRY

Dunkel, a light darker lager with a nutty maltiness, is wonderful with chicken, game birds, and turkey, as is dark and rich **porter.**

FISH

Serve **IPA** with salmon and tuna—or any substantial, meaty fish. **Pale ale** cuts through the oiliness of the fish.

SHELLFISH

The burnt-toast quality of light-in-the-mouth **Irish dry stout** is a wonderful counterpoint to the brininess of shellfish. Irish stouts are famous with oysters.

VEGETABLES

Belgian **dubbel** is rich, without hoppy bitterness, and works well with vegetables. A light **amber ale** will also hold up to grilled vegetables.

SPICY MARINADES

A classic **pilsner** or a **Thai beer,** chilled, has enough bitterness, crispness, and carbonation to hold up to spicy food.

TANGY SAUCES

Flanders brown or **red sour beer** pulls the tang out of the sauce and makes it more potent. A Mexican **lager**, served icy cold, only makes barbecue sauce taste that much better.

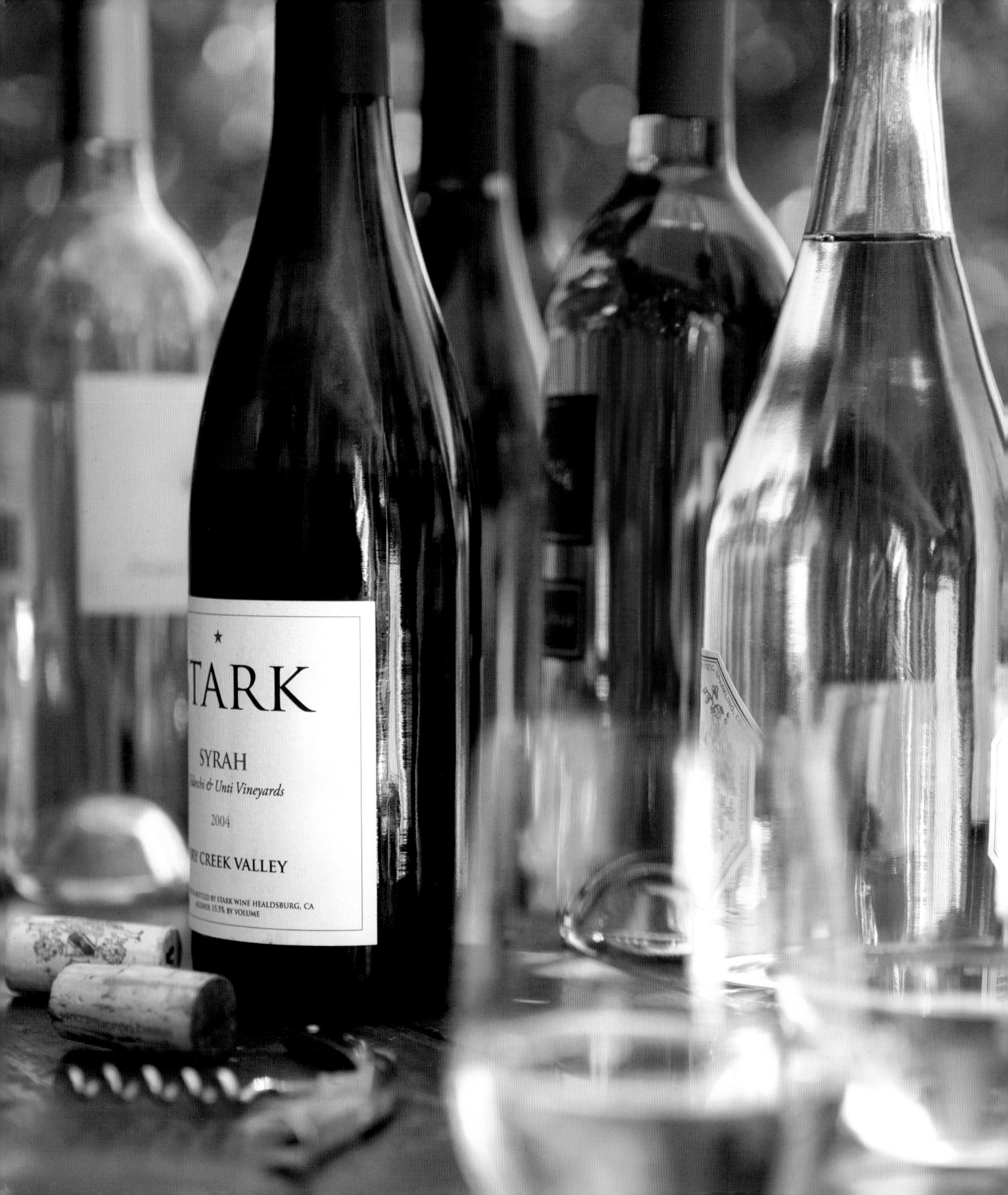
TARK
SYRAH
& Unti Vineyards
2004
CREEK VALLEY

Grilled Foods and Wine

The smoke and spice of many grilled foods can make wine pairing a challenge—but a highly pleasurable one. Happily, the vast world of wine offers tastes that will match any palate and any grilled dish, whether you're looking for a light, simple summer quaffer to serve with a casual barbecue or a serious red to complement an elegant cut of meat.

Wine Pairing Guide

BEEF
Sip a red **Meritage** or a **Cabernet Sauvignon** with big flavors and a tannic finish alongside your steak or burger.

PORK
Since fruit works so well with pork, a jammy, fruit-forward **Zinfandel** would be perfect.

LAMB
Any New World **Shiraz** with a good peppery finish will cut through the fatty richness of lamb.

POULTRY
Chardonnay with little oak works well with simply grilled chicken. A **Viognier** with notes of apricots, peaches, and pears is nice with quail and duck. Turkey is a challenge; most will go with a **Riesling,** but a lighter **Zinfandel** is a surprising change.

FISH
With seafood, try a **Champagne** from the Côtes des Blanc region of France, light and not overpowering, or a standby **Sauvignon Blanc,** with their citrus herbaceous crispness, especially one from California or the Loire Valley. Don't overlook **Pinot Noir**, particularly with salmon and tuna; these wines feature notes of raspberry, strawberry, and plum with a hint of smokiness.

SHELLFISH
Sancerre, with its grapefruity acidity, pairs beautifully with crab. **Muscadet de Servre-et-Maine,** with it's soft and creamy citrus notes, knocks oysters to a different level. With any shellfish, try a good **Chablis,** that is flinty with hints of vanilla.

VEGETABLES
Grüner Veltliner is crisp and slightly spicy, making it a nice choice as the natural sugars of most vegetables come out when grilled. **Sauvignon Blanc** with its herbaceous, grassy notes has long been paired with asparagus and even tomatoes.

SPICY MARINADES
Riesling and **Gewürztraminer** both have a sweet component to offset spiciness. Riesling's peach and floral essence or Gewürztraminer's rose and spice crispness can temper a spicy marinade and let the underlying flavors shine through.

TANGY SAUCES
A **Bandol rosé** is always good with a barbecue sauce; it is even keeled and can handle any sauce you throw at it. A **Barolo** that's at least 5 years old is earthy, with hints of truffles and a bit of chocolate, and sturdy enough to stand tall with a tangy sauce that complements it at the same time.

Adventures in Grilling

Summer Picnic

The glowing sun and the heat of summer entice anyone to enjoy the open air. With an abundance of warmth and light, a picnic is a great way to share a meal with friends and family. Today, grilling is no longer left to the confines of your backyard; with the increasing availability of portable grills, you can easily pack one up to take along wherever you choose. Whether the venue is a meadow, park, or vineyard, all you need to do is to stock your picnic basket, grab the grill, and you're ready to feast on all that summer has to offer.

What's in the Basket

SPARKLING MINT LEMONADE
page 218

NECTARINE & APRICOT SKEWERS
page 64

TURKEY BURGERS
page 154

ORZO SALAD
page 200

ASSORTED CHEESES
page 30

CHEESE COURSE

There are many types of cheeses that are perfect for a summertime picnic. Those with a harder rind will travel well in your cooler. Wrap them in waxed paper or plastic wrap and serve on a wooden board along with bread, crackers, fresh fruit, or nuts.

The Perfect Summer Picnic

Gather ingredients Make a list and shop before your picnic. To keep things simple, use the suggested menu on the previous page, or create your own. Be sure to buy fresh meat and produce that is in season.

Choose the right spot Select a shady location, unless you don't mind a little bit of sun. If you choose a spot in the grass, inspect for poison ivy and poison oak before you set your blanket down. Set up your grill on a concrete or rocky surface; avoid putting it in the grass, where it could easily start a fire.

Start the fire Make sure that you have read your grill's instruction manual on how to properly start it. All you'll need is some charcoal, wood chips, and a fire source and you'll be on your way. See pages 15–16 for more information.

Grill the food Before you set any food down on the grill, make sure the grates are clean to avoid any unwanted flavor. Let the grill heat up before you begin to cook.

Keep the fire going Never leave your grill unattended. Plan to keep your fire going by adding coals when you notice the fire is starting to burn down. If your grill has vents, maintain the temperature range by adjusting them if necessary.

Let the grill cool Before packing up to go home, let your fire die down and make sure the grill has cooled before you pack it up.

A Day at the Lake

Lazy summer days call for staying cool and taking advantage of the great outdoors. What could be better than a day spent at the lake? A freshwater lake offers up the chance to fish and swim, but at the end of the day it also becomes the perfect setting for grilling the day's catch. Bring your portable grill (or use the grill provided if you're in a park), along with the necessary grilling accessories and a cooler full of cold beverages, and you'll have all that you need to dine al fresco at nature's scenic table.

What's for Dinner

FISH ON THE GRILL

CLEAN YOUR CATCH

If you caught your fish, the first step is to clean it. Using the blunt side of a knife, scrape off the scales on the outside. Insert the sharp end of the knife into the belly and make a shallow cut from head to tail. Remove the entrails and bones, if needed. Rinse the fish inside and out.

ADD MORE FLAVOR

Gently holding the back of the cleaned fish, stuff fresh herbs and slices of citrus into the cavity. As the fish cooks on the grill, the flesh will take on the essence of any flavors you add. Try variations of rosemary, thyme, oregano, verbena, and bay leaves mixed with lemon, orange, or lime.

START THE FIRE

Ignite the coals using a chimney starter and then spread the coals two or three layers deep to form an even fire bed on the fire grate. Position the grill rack over the coals. If using a gas grill, light the grill following the manufacturer's instructions 10–15 minutes in advance of cooking.

GRILL YOUR FISH

Cook fresh fish such as trout and striped bass over direct or indirect heat. Make sure the grill rack is as clean as possible, and oiled, to prevent the fish from sticking to it. Lay the fish at a diagonal across the grill and cook, turning once, until opaque throughout, 4–5 minutes per side.

Beach Grilling Party

A day at the beach warrants an oceanside grilling party. Round up your friends, pack up treasures from the sea such as fresh lobster, oysters, or shrimp, and head to the sand. If your beach doesn't allow for a fire pit, bring a portable grill along with all the needed tools and an ice-filled cooler stocked with side dishes, condiments, and beverages. The next step is to light up the coals, kick back, and relax in the sun by the surf. Don't forget your beach chairs!

What's for Dinner

LIVE LOBSTERS

When you purchase lobster, be certain that it is fresh. Look for a lively one with bright, shiny eyes, and a tail that curls and tucks up under its body. Make sure it is wrapped in a thick layer of newspaper or in a paper bag, not in plastic, which can suffocate it. If you catch a live lobster, it's important to cook it within 12 to 18 hours.

Beach Grilling Party

Pack the food With the wide range of coolers available, transporting food is easy. Make sure food that needs to be kept cold, especially seafood, is packed in plenty of ice.

Pick your spot Choose a spot where grilling is allowed. Make sure you're far enough from the water so a rogue wave or the incoming tide can't soak you and your fire. Once you find your spot, set up camp with your grill, blankets, and beach chairs.

Watch the tide Stay far enough from the shore to avoid an incoming tide. If you get too close, a dangerous situation can occur. Check the local news or Internet tide tables to learn when the tide will come in and go out.

Start the fire Bring long matches or a lighter to light your charcoal grill. If possible, place your grill in a spot that is free from wind or has a wind barrier. If you are building a fire pit, clear a space, dig a pit, and place your firewood and kindling in it.

Check the weather Do as the surfers do: Check the weather before you head to the waves. You don't want to prepare for fun in the sun and then be surprised by inclement weather.

Backyard Barbecue

Every serious grill cook looks forward to his or her annual backyard barbecue. It's a time-honored tradition that strikes when the weather is right and the days are long. It's also a time to gather your friends and family, and most importantly, a time to show off your grilling abilities. Pick a sunny day or warm evening, fire up the coals, and take advantage of the bounty of produce that arrives with the summer season.

The Perfect Barbecue

Chill the drinks Few things are better than a frosty beer or ice-cold tea, so keep all drinks on ice and in a shady area.

Get great ingredients Select foods that are in season, such as sweet corn or fresh peaches, and buy locally for the best flavor. When buying meat, choose hormone free and organic whenever possible. Seek out a reputable local butcher.

Keep foods fresh If leaving food out for a long period of time, cover it up with mesh screens to avoid pesky critters and keep out of the sunlight to avoid spoilage. If there is a problem with bugs, set all the food up indoors buffet-style and let guests serve themselves.

Make things comfortable Be sure to have plenty of seats scattered around the yard so everyone has a place to sit.

Set a casual table A backyard barbecue doesn't require your best wares, but have enough plates and utensils for everyone. Place serving spoons and forks alongside your serving bowls and platters.

DRINK STATIONS
Set up satellite drink stations throughout the backyard. Have one that's alcohol free for the little ones, and another with prepared mixed drinks, or a cooler filled with beer, water, and ice. This makes it easy for guests to serve themselves and stay hydrated.

Pig Roast

Spit-roasting a whole 50-pound (25-kg) pig is one memorable, and tasty, grilling adventure—a big project to be undertaken with the help of others. A large pit fire (or large drum barbecue pit) is not something to mess around with, so enlist friends as assistant pit masters. Have them monitor and stoke the fire, help transport and prepare the pig, and assist with getting the pig on and off the fire. Once the pig is done, you won't be able to resist the urge to take decent-size hunks of it while it's still on the spit, nor will your buddies.

What's for Dinner

PERFECT ICED TEA

SONOMA SUCCOTASH SALAD

NEW POTATO SALAD

SPIT-ROASTED PIG

PINEAPPLE SKEWERS WITH RUM & MOLASSES

HOW TO ROAST A PIG

MAKE A PIT

Use a shovel or rake to clear an area to build your own pit. Choose a nonflammable surface such as a steel drum, brick, gravel, or dirt. Line the bottom and sides of the drum or pit with large stones to retain the heat. For more information, see page 13.

START A FIRE

Fill the pit with logs or kindling. Ignite a large bonfire by placing hardwood logs and charcoal in your pit. Light and let burn down 1–2 hours until the embers are covered in ash. Next, place the pig on the rotisserie over the burning fire.

CHECK FOR DONENESS

The pig is done when the skin is golden brown and
crisp. Use a meat thermometer to make sure the internal
temperature is 155–160°F (70–90°C) in the shoulder,
hindquarters, and belly cavity.

CARVE THE PORK

After you have successfully removed the pig from the spit
and onto a table or large work surface, it's ready to be
carved. Using a large carving knife, start at the cheeks and
shoulder and work your way through the ribs and tenderloin
to the hindquarters. Carve against the grain.

Hot-Smoking Salmon

Smoking is a grilling technique that infuses layers of smoky flavor into meat and fish. The trick to the intense flavor is in the slow cooking time. You'll need a grill with a lid, a smoker box or foil packet (if using a gas grill), and wood chips which are necessary for adding the flavor. You can also add nuances with other aromatics such as citrus or fresh herbs like rosemary and thyme. Plan on several hours to smoke foods on the grill before eating them. It takes time, but the results are well worth the effort.

What's for Dinner

ARTICHOKES WITH MEYER LEMON AIOLI
page 72

QUINOA SALAD
page 209

HOME-CURED SMOKED SALMON
page 172

HOW TO SMOKE A FISH ON THE GRILL

ADD FLAVOR

Begin to infuse flavor by adding a brine or a rub to your fish (for more information, see page 172). Rub it into the flesh, cover tightly, and refrigerate for up to 3 hours. Remove from the refrigerator about 30 minutes before you plan on grilling.

WASH AWAY THE BRINE

If you've added a brine or a wet rub, wash it off the fish by putting under running cold water. This step can be skipped if you've added a dry rub or marinade.

SET ON THE GRILL

Place the fish on the grill grate and position the grate so the fish is over the cool side of the grill. Cover the grill and follow the recipe instructions to smoke for several hours.

SERVE IT UP

Once the fish is cooked through and infused with smoky flavor, serve right away. Most smoked foods are so flavorful that they need few accompaniments. Here the salmon is simply served with flatbread crackers and crème fraîche.

Tailgate Party

The art of tailgating is a North American ritual held before a sporting event or rock concert; what was once an underground affair has now become a mainstream event enjoyed by everyone. There are three necessities for successful tailgating: a vehicle with a tailgate, a parking lot, and a grill. If you have these, you're in business. Equally important are the foods that go on the grill and cold beverages of your choice. You can keep this event simple or make it as extravagant as you want.

The Perfect Tailgate

Pack your cooler You'll be transporting perishable food, so make sure your meat and any perishable side dishes are well packed in a cooler filled with ice.

Transport your grill If you're an experienced tailgater and you plan on feeding a crowd, go ahead and pack up your big kettle grill. A smaller, portable grill will also do the job.

Pick your spot Most people tailgate outside of sports arenas in the parking lots. Don't let that stop you, though; you can tailgate anywhere, but be careful to set your grill only on a nonflammable surface.

Be fire safe You will more than likely be in a crowd during your tailgating event, so never leave your grill unattended. Also, be certain that you have successfully put your fire out and that the grill has cooled before you put it back into the car.

Make s'mores Serve items that are easy to make on the grill, such as s'mores. Brown a skewered marshmallow and sandwich it between two graham crackers with a small bar of chocolate, and you have a delicious treat!

THE PERFECT SNACK
For a game-time snack, put popcorn kernels in a loose packet of aluminum foil. Place on the grill over direct heat and let the kernels pop into popcorn. Be careful when you're opening the pack so you don't get steam burns. Top with melted butter, season with flavored salt, and you're ready to go.

Turkey on the Grill

Who says a turkey needs to be cooked in the oven? Throw that old-fashioned notion out the window and enlist your grill to do the cooking. The result will be a deliciously juicy turkey with a crisp skin and smoky flavor. And you'll free up oven space for more side dishes or an additional pie. Just be sure your grill is large enough to house a turkey (a standard kettle grill should do the trick). For maximum flavor potential, brine the turkey for at least 12 hours before it hits the grill; use wood chips such as cherry, hickory, pecan, or maple.

What's for Dinner

SPIKED WARM APPLE CIDER

FENNEL WITH ROMESCO SAUCE
page 76

WILD RICE SALAD
page 208

EGGPLANT, PEPPER & SCALLION SALAD
page 88

GRILLED TURKEY
page 157

GRILLED APPLES WITH ICE CREAM
page 266

Thanksgiving Dinner

Plan the menu The first step in any successful Thanksgiving feast is to have an idea of what you'll be serving. Gather your recipes and make a grocery list before you begin your meal preparation.

Prepare the turkey Leave enough time so that you can brine the turkey for at least 12 hours and plan to cook it for 2½–4 hours with 20–30 minutes of resting time before serving dinner.

Ready the feast Once you have your turkey in the brine, prepare your side dishes, desserts, and any prepared beverages. If time allows, make some items a day ahead and then put them in the oven on Thanksgiving, as this will make the day less hectic.

Set the table Get out your good silverware and plates for this special occasion. If you'll be dining outdoors, a more casual place setting will do. Just be sure you have enough for everyone.

Dine al fresco Weather permitting, have your Thanksgiving dinner outdoors. Dining under colorful foliage in the crisp autumn air makes for a most memorable holiday.

BRINING THE TURKEY

Rinse the turkey, inside and out, under cold running water, then place in the brine. Add cold water to cover the turkey; weigh it down with a plate and refrigerate for up to 12 hours or overnight. Remove the turkey from the brine 1 hour before grilling and pat dry with paper towels. Discard the brine.

Fruits · Vegetables

PEACH, ARUGULA & GOAT CHEESE SALAD

Balsamic vinegar ½ cup
(4 fl oz/125 ml) plus
2 tablespoons

Firm, ripe peaches 2

Light brown sugar
2 tablespoons, firmly packed

Arugula (rocket) 2 bunches
(about 2 cups/2 oz/60 g),
tough stems removed

Grapeseed oil 2 tablespoons

Salt and ground pepper

Fresh goat cheese ¼ lb
(4 oz/125 g), crumbled

This salad showcases ripe peaches in season. Use a local variety of white or yellow peach, or "donut" peaches, which are smaller than regular ones. Balsamic vinegar can be reduced to a syrupy consistency to make a delicious condiment for grilled fruit and salads.

In a saucepan over medium-high heat, bring the ½ cup (4 fl oz/125 ml) vinegar to a boil. Reduce heat to a simmer and cook until thick enough to coat the back of a spoon. Let cool.

Cut the peaches in half lengthwise; remove and discard the pits. Cut each half into 6 wedges. Place the wedges in a shallow dish, sprinkle with the brown sugar, and drizzle with the 2 tablespoons vinegar.

Prepare a **CHARCOAL** or **GAS** grill for **DIRECT** grilling over **MEDIUM-HIGH** heat (pages 15–16). Brush and oil the grill grate or a vegetable-grilling basket.

Arrange the peaches on the grate or in the grilling basket directly over medium-high heat. Grill, turning once, until grill marks appear, about 1 minute per side.

In a large serving bowl, combine the arugula and the oil and toss to coat. Season to taste with salt and pepper.

Arrange the grilled peaches on top of the arugula. Drizzle with the balsamic reduction, sprinkle with the goat cheese, and finish with a few grindings of pepper. Serve at once.

NECTARINE & APRICOT SKEWERS

Alternating nectarine and apricot halves on skewers adds visual interest to this exotic Moroccan combination. Choose fruits that are of similar size and shape. Secure the fruit halves with two skewers to prevent them from rotating.

If you prefer to remove the skins from the fruit, bring a pot three-fourths full of water to a boil. Have ready a bowl full of ice water. Using a paring knife, cut a small X in the skin on the bottom of each nectarine and apricot. Boil the fruits until their skins loosen, about 1 minute. Using a slotted spoon, transfer the fruits to the ice bath. When cool enough to handle, peel the fruits and discard the skins.

Soak the bamboo skewers in water for 30 minutes. Meanwhile, cut the fruits in half lengthwise; remove and discard the pits. Line up the halves on a work surface, alternating between nectarines and apricots. Insert a skewer crosswise through the halves about ½ inch (12 mm) from one end. Insert a second skewer crosswise about ½ inch (12 mm) from the other end.

Prepare a **CHARCOAL** or **GAS** grill for **DIRECT** grilling over **MEDIUM-HIGH** heat (pages 15–16). Brush and oil the grill grate.

Brush the fruit on all sides with oil.

Grill the skewers directly over medium heat, turning once, until grill marks appear and the fruits are slightly soft, about 2–3 minutes per side.

Transfer the skewers to a platter and serve warm.

Firm, ripe nectarines 3

Firm, ripe apricots 4

Grapeseed oil for brushing

Bamboo skewers 12

HOW TO PREVENT BAMBOO SKEWERS FROM BURNING

Before threading bamboo skewers, soak them in water for at least 30 minutes. When placing skewers on the grill, angle the ends towards the edge of the grill, an area of lower heat, or over a piece of foil laid on the grill rack to prevent them from scorching or catching fire.

PINEAPPLE SKEWERS WITH RUM & MOLASSES

MAKES 6–8 SERVINGS

Pineapples are a tropical treat any time of year and grilling is a fun way to prepare them. Skewered with their spiny tops still intact, they make attractive accompaniments to grilled sausages, pork tenderloin, and fish. Look for medium-sized, firm pineapples with brightly colored skins such as the Maui Gold variety.

Soak the bamboo skewers in water for 30 minutes.

In a small saucepan over medium heat, whisk together the molasses, agave syrup, and rum. Bring to a boil and simmer until reduced slightly, 3–4 minutes.

Using a serrated knife, cut the pineapple in half lengthwise. Cut each half lengthwise into 6 wedges; cut away and discard the core from each wedge. Place the wedges, skin side down, on a cutting board. Working with one wedge at a time, carefully run the knife between the skin and the flesh to separate the flesh. Cut the flesh crosswise into 6 chunks. Thread each row of chunks onto a skewer.

Prepare a **CHARCOAL** or **GAS** grill for **DIRECT** grilling over **HIGH** heat (pages 15–16). Brush and oil the grill grate.

Brush the fruit on all sides with oil and sprinkle with the sugar.

Grill the skewers directly over high heat, turning once, until grill marks appear, about 4 minutes per side.

Transfer the skewers to a large serving platter and drizzle with the rum and molasses syrup. Serve at once.

Molasses 2 tablespoons

Light agave syrup or honey 2 tablespoons

Dark rum 2 tablespoons

Pineapple 1

Grapeseed oil for brushing

Sugar 3 tablespoons

Bamboo skewers 12

PEAR & WATERCRESS SALAD

Champagne Vinaigrette
(page 260)

Vanilla bean 1

Firm, ripe pears such as
Bartlett (Williams') or Anjou 3

White wine 3 cups (24 fl oz/
750 ml)

Granulated sugar 1 cup
(8 oz/250 g)

Lavender or regular honey
2 tablespoons

Watercress 3 bunches (about
3–4 cups/3–4 oz/90–120 g),
tough stems removed

Salt and cracked pepper

Grapeseed oil for brushing

Walnut halves ½ cup (2 oz/
60 g), toasted

Unless they are perfectly ripe, most pears require poaching prior to grilling to soften them. Store-bought poached pears in light syrup are an easy alternative. Watercress is a spicy salad green that is available in spring and summer.

Split the vanilla bean lengthwise and scrape out the seeds into a small bowl; reserve the pod.

Peel the pears, cut in half lengthwise, and core. Set aside.

In a saucepan over medium-high heat, whisk together the wine, sugar, honey, and vanilla seeds and pod until the sugar and honey dissolve, about 10 minutes. Add the pear halves and enough water to cover them completely. Cut out a parchment paper circle with a center vent and fit it inside the pan, covering the surface of the poaching liquid. Bring the liquid to a boil and skim the surface to remove any foam. Reduce the heat to a simmer and cook the pears until there is little resistance when pierced with the tip of a knife, about 5 minutes. Let the pears cool in the syrup.

In a large bowl, combine the watercress and half of the champagne vinaigrette and toss to coat. Season to taste with salt and ground pepper. Divide the watercress among serving plates.

Prepare a **CHARCOAL** or **GAS** grill for **DIRECT** grilling over **MEDIUM-HIGH** heat (pages 15–16). Brush and oil the grill grate.

Remove the pears from the syrup and pat dry with paper towels. Generously season the inside of the pear halves with pepper, gently pressing the pepper into the surface of the pears. Brush the peppered side with oil.

Grill the pear halves, peppered side down, directly over medium-high heat until grill marks appear, about 2 minutes.

Transfer the pears to a cutting board and let cool slightly. Thinly slice the grilled pear halves lengthwise. Arrange the slices on top of the watercress, drizzle with the remaining vinaigrette, and garnish with the toasted walnut halves. Serve.

WATERMELON WITH MINT ZABAGLIONE

MINT ZABAGLIONE

Large egg yolks 4

Granulated sugar ½ cup
(4 oz/125 g)

Salt

Marsala wine ¼ cup
(2 fl oz/125 ml)

Fresh mint leaves 12, rolled up
lengthwise and sliced crosswise
into thin ribbons

Watermelon cut into cubes
1-inch (2.5-cm) thick, rind
removed

Granulated sugar 2 tablespoons

Zest and juice of 1 lime

A favorite summer fruit, watermelon takes on an unexpected flavor profile when grilled. Mint-flavored zabaglione transforms the fruit from a backyard barbecue staple into a dressed-up southern Italian showstopper. At the height of the season, substitute honeydew melon or cantaloupe for the watermelon.

To make the mint zabaglione, in a heatproof bowl or the top of a double-boiler, whisk together the egg yolks, ½ cup sugar, and a pinch of salt until thick and pale colored, about 2 minutes. Place the bowl over (not touching) barely simmering water. Continue whisking until the mixture doubles in volume and registers 110°F (43°C) on an instant-read thermometer, about 10 minutes. Add the wine and continue whisking vigorously until the mixture triples in volume and no liquid remains in the bottom of the bowl, about 10 minutes. Fold in the mint. Transfer the zabaglione to a serving bowl and let stand at room temperature or cover and refrigerate until chilled.

Prepare a **CHARCOAL** or **GAS** grill for **DIRECT** grilling over **MEDIUM** heat (pages 15–16). Brush and oil the grill grate.

Grill the watermelon cubes over the hottest part of the fire until grill marks appear, about 2 minutes. Turn the cubes over and grill again until marks appear, about 2 minutes longer. Repeat the process on all sides.

Place the watermelon cubes in a bowl. Add the 2 tablespoons sugar and the lime zest and juice and gently toss to coat.

Divide the watermelon among serving plates and top with the zabaglione.

FIGS WRAPPED IN PROSCIUTTO

When Mission figs are in season in summer, there is no better time to showcase their delicate and refined flavor. They are an excellent accompaniment to chicken and pork. Grilled stuffed figs make fine passed hors d'oeuvres.

Trim off the stem ends of the figs. Cut the figs in half or quarters lengthwise, depending on their size. Lay the prosciutto slices flat on a work surface. With a sharp knife, cut each slice crosswise into 4 pieces. Spoon 1 teaspoonful of goat cheese on top of each fig and tightly wrap with a piece of prosciutto. Secure the bundles with toothpicks, if necessary.

Prepare a **CHARCOAL** or **GAS** grill for **DIRECT** grilling over **MEDIUM-HIGH** heat (pages 15–16). Brush and oil the grill grate.

Lightly brush the fig bundles with oil and season with salt and pepper.

Grill the bundles directly over medium-high heat, turning often, until well marked on all sides, about 4–6 minutes. Move the bundles to indirect heat and drizzle with the balsamic vinegar. Grill, covered, until figs are cooked through and the cheese melts, about 3 minutes longer.

Transfer the fig bundles to a serving platter, drizzle with the honey, and serve hot.

Mission figs 4

Parma prosciutto 4–6 slices

Fresh goat cheese ¼ cup (1¼ oz/30 g), at room temperature

Olive oil for brushing

Salt and ground pepper

Balsamic vinegar or balsamic syrup (see note) 2 tablespoons

Lavender honey 2 tablespoons

HOW TO MAKE A BALSAMIC SYRUP

If you don't have best-quality aged balsamic vinegar on hand, you can make your own balsamic syrup to approximate it. In a small saucepan over medium-high heat, combine 1 cup (8 fl oz/250 ml) balsamic vinegar and 2 tablespoons light agave syrup and bring to a boil. Reduce the heat to low and simmer until the syrup is thick enough to coat the back of a spoon, about 2 minutes. Let cool. Use balsamic syrup as a condiment with grilled fruits, vegetables, and salads.

RADICCHIO SALAD

Balsamic vinegar
2 tablespoons

Light agave syrup or honey
1 tablespoon

Radicchio 2–3 heads

Juice of 1 lemon

Olive oil 2 tablespoons

Salt and ground pepper

Extra-virgin olive oil 1–2
tablespoons

**Grana padano or pecorino
romano cheese** 1 small chunk,
about 4 oz/125 g

**Fresh flat-leaf (Italian)
parsley** 2 tablespoons, minced

Radicchio is often used in salads for color but can be quite bitter on its own when raw. In the summer when it is plentiful, Italian cooks enjoy grilling radicchio, which helps to soften some of the bitterness. Look for the longer and less bitter Treviso radicchio at farmers' markets.

In a saucepan over medium-high heat, combine the vinegar and agave syrup and bring to a boil. Reduce the heat to low and simmer until slightly thickened, about 2 minutes. Let cool.

Peel away the outer leaves from the radicchio heads and discard. Cut the heads in half lengthwise, and then cut each half into wedges 1½ inches (4 cm) thick. Trim away some of the core from each wedge, leaving the leaves attached at the base.

In a large bowl, combine the radicchio, lemon juice, olive oil, and one-half of the balsamic syrup mixture. Toss to coat and season with salt and pepper. Let stand for 10 minutes.

Prepare a **CHARCOAL** or **GAS** grill for **DIRECT** grilling over **MEDIUM-HIGH** heat (pages 15–16). Brush and oil the grill grate.

Grill the radicchio directly over medium-high heat, turning often, until nicely charred on all sides, about 3–5 minutes.

Transfer the grilled radicchio to a shallow dish and drizzle with the remaining balsamic syrup and the extra-virgin olive oil. Using a vegetable peeler, shave the cheese over the top. Sprinkle with the parsley and serve at once, hot off the grill, or at room temperature.

ARTICHOKES WITH MEYER LEMON AIOLI

Fresh "baby" artichokes are available in spring and early summer. Peel, trim, and parboil them before grilling to soften them. If fresh baby artichokes are not available, you can use store-bought imported artichokes packed in oil, but be sure to drain them well.

Cut 1 of the lemons into quarters; halve and juice the remaining lemon and set aside. Fill a large saucepan three-fourths full of water. Have ready a bowl full of ice water. Add the lemon quarters, garlic, 1 tablespoon salt, and the peppercorns to the saucepan.

Snap off the tough outer leaves of the artichokes to reveal the pale inner leaves. Using a serrated knife, trim off ½ inch (12 mm) of the spiky tips. With a paring knife, cut off the stems ½ inch (12 cm) from the bottom and peel the remaining stems. Working with one artichoke at a time, cut them in half lengthwise and add to the lemon water in the saucepan.

Cut out a parchment paper circle with a center vent and fit it inside the pan. Bring to a boil over high heat. Reduce the heat to medium-low and simmer until tender, 8–10 minutes. Using a slotted spoon, transfer the artichokes to the ice bath. Drain and let dry on paper towels.

In a large bowl, stir together the olive oil, lemon juice, and oregano. Add the artichokes and toss to coat. Season with salt and pepper. Let stand for 20–30 minutes.

Prepare a **CHARCOAL** or **GAS** grill for **DIRECT** grilling over **MEDIUM-HIGH** heat (pages 15–16). Brush and oil the grill grate or a vegetable-grilling basket.

Arrange the artichokes on the grate or in the basket directly over medium-high heat. Grill, turning often, until lightly charred on all sides and tender-crisp, 6–8 minutes.

Arrange the grilled artichokes on a platter and serve hot off the grill with the Meyer lemon aioli on the side.

Meyer Lemon Aioli (page 256)

Lemons 2

Garlic 3 cloves

Salt and ground pepper

Black peppercorns 4

Small artichokes 15–20

Extra-virgin olive oil ¼ cup (2 fl oz/60 ml)

Dried oregano 1 tablespoon

ASPARAGUS WITH SAFFRON AIOLI

Saffron Aioli (page 257)

Medium or thick asparagus
1½ lb (750 g)

Olive oil ¼ cup (2 fl oz/60 ml)

Garlic 2 cloves, slivered

Zest and juice of 1 lemon

Salt and ground pepper

Large eggs 2, hard-boiled

Asparagus spears are fantastic on the grill, which turns the flower ends crispy and charred while the stems remain tender. Saffron aioli adds a distinctive Mediterranean flair. Choose medium or thick asparagus spears; pencil-thin asparagus is hard to handle on the grill and burns easily.

Trim or snap off the tough ends of asparagus, leaving the spear about 5 inches (13 cm) long. Using a vegetable peeler, peel the outer skin, starting 1 inch (2.5 cm) below the tip.

In a shallow dish, stir together the oil, garlic, and lemon zest and juice. Add the asparagus, turn to coat, and season with salt and pepper. Let stand for 10 minutes.

Prepare a **CHARCOAL** or **GAS** grill for **DIRECT** grilling over **MEDIUM-HIGH** heat (pages 15–16). Brush and oil the grill grate.

Grill the asparagus directly over medium-high heat, turning often, until the spears are tender-crisp and grill marks appear, 5–6 minutes.

Peel and halve the hard-boiled eggs. Remove the yolks and finely chop the yolks and whites separately.

Transfer the asparagus to a platter and garnish with alternating bands of the chopped egg yolks and whites. Serve hot off the grill or at room temperature with the saffron aioli on the side.

FENNEL WITH ROMESCO SAUCE

Fennel is a strong licorice-flavored herb that mellows in intensity when grilled. Romesco sauce is a versatile Spanish condiment for many grilled foods, including fish and vegetables.

Trim off the stalks ½ inch (12 mm) above the fennel bulbs, reserving a few green fronds, if any, for garnish. Trim away any bruised skin. Slice the fennel bulbs lengthwise into quarters, trimming away the thickest part of the central core but keeping the layers intact and attached. In a large bowl, combine the fennel and oil and toss to coat. Season with salt and pepper.

Soak the chiles in warm water until soft and pliable, about 10 minutes. Strain and reserve the soaking liquid, and pat dry. Halve and seed the chiles.

Prepare a **CHARCOAL** or **GAS** grill for **DIRECT** grilling over **MEDIUM-HIGH** heat (pages 15–16). Brush and oil the grill grate or a vegetable-grilling basket.

Brush the chiles, bell pepper, tomatoes, onion, and garlic with oil. Arrange the fennel, chiles, bell pepper, tomatoes, onion, and garlic on the grill or in the grilling basket. Grill directly over medium-high heat, turning often, until lightly charred on all sides, 10–15 minutes for the fennel, about 5 minutes for the chile, 8–10 minutes for the bell pepper, 6–8 minutes for the tomatoes, 8–10 minutes for the onion, and 2–3 minutes for the garlic. Transfer to a bowl, cover, and let steam for 10 minutes.

Transfer the grilled fennel to a serving platter.

To make the romesco sauce, using your fingers or a paring knife, peel the bell pepper and tomatoes and discard the skins. In a blender or a food processor, combine the bell pepper, tomatoes, chiles, onion, garlic, almonds, vinegar, wine, and paprika. Process into a pourable sauce, adding the reserved soaking liquid from the chiles as needed. Taste and adjust the seasoning with salt and pepper. Spoon into a serving bowl and serve with the fennel.

Fennel bulbs 2 large

Olive oil ¼ cup (2 fl oz/60 ml), plus oil for brushing

Salt and ground pepper

ROMESCO SAUCE
Añora, ancho, or pasilla chiles 2 dried

Red bell pepper (capsicum) 1, quartered lengthwise and seeded

Plum tomatoes 2, quartered and seeded

Yellow onion 1, quartered

Garlic 4 cloves, peeled

Slivered blanched almonds ¼ cup (1 oz/30 g)

Sherry vinegar 2 tablespoons

White wine 2 tablespoons

Spanish smoked paprika 2 teaspoons

Salt and ground pepper

SONOMA SUCCOTASH SALAD

Champagne Vinaigrette
(page 260)

Sweet corn 6 ears

Unsalted butter 3–4
tablespoons, melted

Salt and ground pepper

Fresh fava beans in their pods
1½ lb (750 g)

Chickpeas (garbanzo beans)
and lima beans 1 can
(15 oz/470 g) *each,* drained
and rinsed

Vine-ripened tomatoes 3,
seeded and diced

Teardrop heirloom tomatoes
10–12, halved lengthwise

Fresh basil, chervil, flat-leaf
(Italian) parsley, and tarragon
2 tablespoons *each,* chopped

Red onion ½ cup (2 oz/60 g),
thinly sliced

Butter (Boston) lettuce 1 head,
torn into large, cup-shaped
pieces

Combining grilled sweet corn with fresh beans makes a succotash far beyond what we remember from the grade school cafeteria. If fresh fava beans are not available, substitute precooked shelled edamame beans (baby soybeans).

Shuck the corn; discard the husks and silk. Soak the corn in ice water to cover for 10 minutes. Drain the corn and pat dry with paper towels. Brush the corn with some of the melted butter and season with salt and pepper.

Bring a pot three-fourths full of salted water to a boil. Have ready a bowl full of ice water. Shuck the fava beans from their outer pods. Boil the favas until their skins loosen, 1–2 minutes. Drain. Plunge the favas into the ice bath and drain again. When cool enough to handle, pinch one end of the favas to squeeze them from their tough outer skins; discard the skins.

Prepare a **CHARCOAL** or **GAS** grill for **DIRECT** grilling over **MEDIUM-HIGH** heat (pages 15–16). Brush and oil the grill grate.

Grill the corn directly over medium-high heat, turning often and basting with the butter, until lightly charred and caramelized on all sides, about 20 minutes.

Transfer the corn to a cutting board and let cool just until it can be handled. Working with one ear at a time, stand the corn, stem end down, on the board and cut the kernels away from the cob in a downward motion.

In a large bowl, combine the corn kernels, favas, chickpeas, lima beans, vine-ripened and teardrop tomatoes, basil, chervil, parsley, tarragon, and onion. Drizzle with ¼ cup (2 fl oz/60 ml) of the champagne vinaigrette and toss gently to coat. Taste and adjust the seasoning with salt and pepper.

Arrange the lettuce leaves into a bed on a serving platter or individual salad plates. Spoon the succotash on top of the lettuce and serve with the remaining vinaigrette on the side.

SUMMER SQUASH SALAD

Zucchini, yellow crookneck, and pattypan squashes are terrific grilled and lightly dressed with a tomato-basil vinaigrette. When shopping for squash, choose a variety of shapes, colors, and sizes.

Cut the zucchini and squashes in half lengthwise, and then cut each half into wedges about ¾ inch (2 cm) thick. In a large bowl, combine the squash wedges, tomatoes, olive oil, and marjoram and toss to coat. Season with the salt and pepper.

Prepare a **CHARCOAL** or **GAS** grill for **DIRECT** grilling over **MEDIUM-HIGH** heat (pages 15–16). Brush and oil the grill grate or a vegetable-grilling basket.

Arrange the squashes and tomatoes on the rack or in the basket directly over medium-high heat. Grill, turning as needed, until lightly charred on all sides, about 8–10 minutes. Move the vegetables to the edge of the grill where the heat is less intense, cover, and grill until cooked through, 5–6 minutes longer.

Transfer the grilled vegetables back to the bowl. Stir in the pine nuts and parsley. Taste and adjust the seasoning.

In a separate medium bowl, season the field greens with salt and pepper and dress with 2 tablespoons tomato-basil vinaigrette. Divide the field greens among 6 serving plates and arrange the grilled vegetables on top. Pass the remaining vinaigrette at the table.

Tomato-Basil Vinaigrette (page 261)

Zucchini (courgettes)
5–6 small to medium (about 2 lb/500 g total weight)

Yellow crookneck squash 5–6, about 2 lb (500 g) total weight

Pattypan squash 10, about 2 lb (500 g) total weight

Plum (Roma) tomatoes 2, cored, quartered, and seeded

Olive oil ½ cup (4 fl oz/ 125 ml)

Fresh marjoram 1 tablespoon minced

Coarse salt 2 teaspoons

Ground pepper 1 teaspoon

Pine nuts ¼ cup (1½ oz/45 g), toasted

Flat-leaf (Italian) parsley 2 tablespoons minced

Field greens or baby lettuce leaves 5 cups (5 oz/150 g)

PORTOBELLO MUSHROOMS WITH HERBED AIOLI

HERBED AIOLI

Grapeseed oil ½ cup (4 fl oz/ 125 ml)

Olive oil ¼ cup (2 fl oz/60 ml)

Egg yolks 2 large

Dijon mustard 2 tablespoons

Garlic 3 cloves

Fresh rosemary and sage 1 tablespoon *each*, minced

Salt ½ teaspoon

Ground white pepper ¼ teaspoon

Portobello mushrooms 6, brushed clean

Olive oil ½ cup (4 fl oz/ 125 ml)

Balsamic vinegar 2 tablespoons

Garlic 2 cloves, minced

Fresh rosemary and sage 1 tablespoon *each*, minced

Salt and ground black pepper

Grill portobellos as you would a steak, with an oil and herb marinade for moisture and flavor, seared with grill marks on the outside, soft and tender on the inside. Here, a strong herbed aioli boosts the flavor of these robust grilled mushrooms.

To make the herbed aioli, combine the grapeseed and olive oils in a glass measuring cup with a spout. In a blender or food processor, combine the egg yolks, mustard, garlic, rosemary, sage, salt, and white pepper. Pulse several times until the garlic is pulverized. With the motor running, add the oil in a slow, steady stream. Stir in cold water, 1 teaspoon at a time, as needed to thin the aioli; it should be the consistency of mayonnaise. Spoon into a serving bowl, cover, and refrigerate for at least 10 minutes.

Trim off all but ½ inch (2 cm) of the stems from the mushrooms. Using a large spoon, scrape the dark gills from the underside of the mushrooms. In a shallow dish, stir together the oil, vinegar, garlic, rosemary, and sage. Add the mushrooms and turn to coat. Season with salt and black pepper. Let stand for 10–15 minutes.

Prepare a **CHARCOAL** or **GAS** grill for **DIRECT** grilling over **MEDIUM-HIGH** heat (pages 15–16). Brush and oil the grill grate.

Grill the mushrooms directly over medium-high heat, turning often, until grill marks appear, 3–4 minutes. Move the mushrooms to the edge of the grill where the heat is less intense and brush with the remaining marinade. Cover and grill until the mushrooms are slightly soft and cooked through, 3–4 minutes longer.

Transfer the grilled mushrooms to a cutting board and slice on the diagonal. Serve at once with the herbed aioli on the side.

CORN WITH SORGHUM BUTTER

For American grilling enthusiasts, grilled fresh corn on the cob with a dollop of flavored butter is the ultimate roll-up-your-sleeves-and-dig-in kind of food. It can be a generous side dish to fish, meat, or poultry on the grill.

To make the sorghum butter, whisk the butter in a bowl until smooth. Whisk in the lemon juice and a pinch of salt. Add the syrup in a slow, steady stream, whisking constantly, until incorporated. Scrape the butter onto a piece of parchment (baking) paper and shape into a rough log. Fold the paper over the butter, rolling it gently to close. Press a ruler against the seam and pull the loose end of paper while applying pressure against the ruler to form the butter into a straight log. Refrigerate the log for 30 minutes or freeze for 10 minutes.

Shuck the corn; discard the husks and silk. Soak the corn in ice water to cover for 10 minutes. Drain the corn and pat dry with paper towels. Brush with some of the melted butter and season with salt and pepper.

Prepare a **CHARCOAL** or **GAS** grill for **DIRECT** grilling over **MEDIUM-HIGH** heat (pages 15–16). Brush and oil the grill grate.

Grill the corn directly over medium-high heat, turning often and basting as needed with the butter, until lightly charred and caramelized on all sides, about 20 minutes.

Transfer the grilled corn to a platter. Unwrap the sorghum butter, place it on a butter dish, and serve with the hot corn.

SORGHUM BUTTER

Unsalted butter 1 cup (8 oz/250 g), at room temperature

Juice of 1 lemon

Salt

Sweet sorghum syrup or molasses 2 tablespoons

Fresh sweet corn 6 ears

Unsalted butter 3 tablespoons, melted

Salt and ground pepper

PANZANELLA SALAD

Balsamic Vinaigrette
(page 261)

Heirloom tomatoes 6, about
3 lb (1.5 g) total weight

Small pear-shaped heirloom
tomatoes 1 pint (12 oz/375 g)

Salt and ground pepper

Rosemary focaccia 6 slices

Olive oil for brushing

Garlic 6 cloves

Balsamic vinegar ¼ cup
(2 fl oz/60 ml)

Fresh basil 10 leaves, rolled
lengthwise and sliced crosswise
into ribbons

Fresh flat-leaf (Italian)
parsley 3 tablespoons minced

Arugula (rocket) 3 cups
(3 oz/90 g), tough stems removed

Romaine (cos) lettuce hearts
2 cups (2 oz/60 g), cut into
¾-inch (2-cm) chunks

Red onion 1, thinly sliced

Nothing goes to waste in the Italian kitchen, including slightly stale bread. Day-old bread is preferred for this typical Italian summer salad. The recipe calls for rosemary focaccia, but you can substitute any good-quality artisan country or sourdough bread.

Cut the heirloom and pear-shaped tomatoes in half. Place the tomatoes in a colander over a bowl and generously season with salt. Let stand for 10 minutes to drain, and reserve the liquid released by the tomatoes.

Prepare a **CHARCOAL** or **GAS** grill for **DIRECT** grilling over **MEDIUM-HIGH** heat (pages 15–16). Brush and oil the grill grate.

Brush the focaccia slices with oil. Grill the focaccia directly over medium-high heat turning once, until nicely charred, about 4–5 minutes per side.

Transfer the focaccia to a cutting board. Let cool slightly. Tear or cut the grilled focaccia into ¾-inch (2-cm) chunks.

With the flat side of a chef's knife, crush the garlic cloves into a paste.

In a large bowl, stir together the reserved liquid, vinegar, ¼ cup (2 fl oz/60 ml) water, and 1 tablespoon of the balsamic vinaigrette. Add the garlic and grilled bread chunks and toss to soak the bread. Add the tomatoes, basil, and parsley. Taste and adjust the seasoning and toss again.

In another large bowl, combine the arugula, romaine, and red onion and season with salt and pepper. Add the balsamic vinaigrette, 1 tablespoon at a time, and toss to coat. Add the tomato and bread mixture and toss again.

Mound the salad in a large serving bowl or divide evenly among individual salad plates and serve at once.

EGGPLANT, PEPPER & SCALLION SALAD

This vegetable salad is influenced by the flavors of the Mediterranean. Salting eggplants before grilling helps them to release liquid and rids them of any bitterness. If you are pressed for time, omit this step.

In a bowl, combine the olive oil, garam masala, thyme, basil, and a pinch each of salt and pepper.

With a sharp knife, trim off the tops of the eggplants. Using a vegetable peeler, remove vertical strips of the skin in a striped pattern. Cut the eggplant into rounds ½ inch (12 mm) thick. Arrange the rounds in a single layer on a paper towel–lined baking sheet and generously season both sides with salt and pepper. Let stand for 30 minutes to drain eggplant.

In a bowl, combine the bell peppers, chiles, and ¼ cup (2 fl oz/60 ml) of the spiced oil, and toss to coat.

Brush the scallions with the spiced oil. Brush both sides of the eggplant rounds with the spiced oil and season with salt and pepper.

Prepare a **CHARCOAL** or **GAS** grill for **DIRECT** grilling over **HIGH** heat (pages 15–16). Brush and oil the grill grate or a vegetable-grilling basket.

Working in batches, arrange the bell peppers, chiles, scallions, and eggplant rounds on the grill rack or in the grilling basket directly over high heat. Grill the vegetables, turning often, until nicely charred on all sides, about 6–8 minutes for the bell peppers, 8–10 minutes for the chiles, 2–3 minutes for the scallions, and 8–10 minutes for the eggplant. As they become tender, move the vegetables to the edge of the grill where the heat is less intense and grill until cooked through, 20–30 minutes total, depending on the type of vegetable.

Transfer the vegetables to a large serving platter and serve at once.

Olive oil 1 cup (8 fl oz/250 ml)

Garam masala 2 teaspoons

Dried thyme 1 teaspoon

Dried basil 1 teaspoon

Salt and ground pepper

Eggplants (aubergines) 2 medium

Red bell peppers (capsicums) 2, seeded and cut lengthwise into thin strips

Yellow bell peppers (capsicums) 2, seeded and cut lengthwise into thin strips

Orange bell peppers (capsicums) 2, seeded and cut lengthwise into thin strips

Anaheim chiles 4, halved lengthwise and seeded

Scallions (green or spring onions) 10, trimmed, including 3 inches (7.5 cm) of tender green tops

NEW POTATO SALAD

Small new potatoes
4 lb (2 kg)

Olive oil for brushing

White wine such as Sauvignon Blanc ¼ cup (2 fl oz/60 ml), plus 2 tablespoons

Sea salt and ground pepper

Mayonnaise ½ cup (1½ oz/45 g)

Whole-grain mustard
1 teaspoon

Fresh flat-leaf (Italian) parsley 2 tablespoons minced

Fresh tarragon 2 tablespoons minced

Fresh chives 2 tablespoons finely chopped

Here's a new variation on potato salad. Potatoes are grilled and then tossed with the dressing while they are still warm, which helps them to absorb more flavor. Pack up this salad and take it with you on a picnic or wherever you'll be doing your outdoor grilling.

Bring a saucepan three-fourths full of water to a boil. Add the potatoes and parboil just until they can be pierced with a knife but are not completely tender, 5–7 minutes. Drain and pat dry. Brush the potatoes with olive oil.

Prepare a **CHARCOAL** or **GAS** grill for **DIRECT** grilling over **MEDIUM-HIGH** heat (pages 15–16). Brush and oil the grill grate.

Grill the potatoes over the hottest part of the fire, turning once or twice, until tender when pierced with the tip of a knife, 4–5 minutes.

Transfer the potatoes to a cutting board, let cool just until they can be handled, and then slice or cut into chunks, discarding the small end pieces. Transfer the potatoes to a large bowl while still warm; add the ½ cup (4 fl oz/125 ml) white wine and salt and pepper to taste. Toss gently to coat. Let stand until completely cool, 20–30 minutes, or refrigerate until needed, up to 2 days. (The potatoes will absorb most of the wine.)

To make the dressing, mix together the mayonnaise, the 2 tablespoons white wine, mustard, salt, pepper, and herbs. Add the dressing to the potatoes and toss to coat.

Serve at once or tightly cover and refrigerate for up to 2 days.

GRILLED GAZPACHO

Grilling the vegetables for a cold gazpacho adds an unexpected depth of flavor. This summer soup tastes best when prepared a day in advance, chilled overnight to meld the flavors together, and finished with fresh herbs at the table.

Core, quarter, and seed the plum and heirloom tomatoes. Place the tomatoes in a colander over a bowl and sprinkle with salt. Let stand for 10 minutes. Transfer the water drained from the tomatoes to a sealed container, cover, and refrigerate.

Prepare a **CHARCOAL** or **GAS** grill for **DIRECT** grilling over **MEDIUM-HIGH** heat (pages 15–16). Brush and oil the grill grate or a vegetable-grilling basket.

Brush the zucchini, tomatoes, bell peppers, and chiles with olive oil and lightly season with salt and pepper.

Working in batches, arrange the zucchini, tomatoes, bell peppers, and chiles on the grate or in the basket directly over medium-high heat. Grill, turning frequently, until soft and nicely charred on all sides, about 2–4 minutes total for the zucchini and 10 minutes total for the tomatoes, bell peppers, and chiles.

Transfer the grilled vegetables to a platter and let cool slightly. Pick over the vegetables, removing most of the burned skin but leaving some charred bits.

Working in batches, in a blender or food processor, combine the grilled vegetables, half of the cucumbers, and the hot-pepper sauce, and process until puréed. Add ½ cup (4 fl oz/125 ml) of the tomato soup or more as needed to thin the purée to a pourable consistency. Taste and adjust the seasoning; the gazpacho should be highly seasoned and spicy. Transfer to a glass pitcher, cover, and refrigerate for at least 2 hours or preferably overnight.

To serve, fill individual clear shot glasses or espresso cups three-fourths full with the gazpacho. Top each with 1 teaspoon of the remaining cucumbers, 1 tablespoon of the reserved tomato water, 3 drops extra-virgin olive oil, and a pinch of the fresh herbs. Serve at once.

Ingredients

Plum (Roma) tomatoes 6

Heirloom tomatoes 4

Salt and ground pepper

Olive oil for brushing

Zucchini (courgettes) 2 small, sliced lengthwise into strips ¼ inch (6 mm) thick

Red bell peppers (capsicums) 2, halved lengthwise and seeded

Jalapeño chiles 2, halved lengthwise and seeded

English (hothouse) cucumbers 2, peeled, seeded, and chopped

Hot-pepper sauce 1 tablespoon

Tomato soup 4 cups (32 fl oz/1 l)

Extra-virgin olive oil for drizzling

Fresh chives, chervil, flat-leaf (Italian) parsley, and tarragon 1 tablespoon *each*, chopped and mixed together

ANTIPASTO GRILL

Sea salt and cracked pepper

Eggplants 2, cut crosswise into slices ½ inch (12 mm) thick

Olive oil 1½ cups (12 fl oz/375 ml)

Mixed fresh herbs 8 tablespoons chopped, plus extra for garnish

Garlic 4 cloves, minced, plus 2–3 medium heads, ½ inch (12 mm) of top trimmed

Balsamic vinegar

Red and yellow bell peppers (capsicums) 2 each, seeded and cut lengthwise into strips

Mild green chiles 4–6, halved lengthwise and seeded

Asparagus 1½ lb (750 g), trimmed

Sweet onions 2, halved and peeled

Green (spring) onions 6, trimmed, including 2–3 inches (5–7.5 cm) of tender green tops

Yellow squash and zucchini (courgettes) 2 or 3 each, trimmed and halved lengthwise, flesh lightly scored

Tomatoes 4–6, cut into wedges

Mixed oil-cured olives 1 cup (6 oz/180 g)

Due to the large amount of vegetables and the long cooking time, be prepared to replenish the coals every 20–30 minutes if using a charcoal grill, or have a back-up tank at the ready if using a gas grill. Use fresh herbs such as rosemary, thyme, oregano, and marjoram. Serve with slices of grilled coarse country bread, if you like.

Salt the eggplants and let them drain in a colander.

To make an herbed oil, in a bowl, combine the oil, mixed fresh herbs, minced garlic, 1 tablespoon salt, and 1 teaspoon pepper.

Prepare a **CHARCOAL** or **GAS** grill for **DIRECT** grilling over **MEDIUM-HIGH** heat (pages 15–16). Brush and oil the grill grate.

Set the garlic heads on aluminum foil, and drizzle with 1–2 tablespoons of the herbed oil and a few drops of vinegar. Season with salt and pepper and seal the foil tightly.

Place the garlic heads near the edge of the grill where the heat is less intense and grill, checking occasionally and being careful not to burn them, until soft and caramelized, 10–12 minutes. Meanwhile, working in batches, arrange the eggplant, bell peppers, chiles, asparagus, sweet and green onions, squash, and zucchini on the grill grate over the hottest part of the fire. Brush the vegetables with the herbed oil and grill, turning often, until grill marks appear, about 5 minutes, depending on the type of vegetable. Move the vegetables to the edge of the grill where the heat is less intense and grill until tender-crisp, about 5 minutes longer, depending on the type of vegetable.

Transfer the grilled vegetables to a large platter and garnish with fresh herbs. Serve the antipasto with the tomatoes, olives, and roasted garlic and best-quality aged balsamic vinegar and the roasted garlic.

Beef • Pork • Lamb

SKIRT STEAK FAJITAS

Olive oil ¼ cup (2 fl oz/60 ml)

Small onion 1, minced

Garlic 2 cloves, minced

Red wine vinegar
3 tablespoons

Chile powder and ground cumin 1 teaspoon *each*

Salt and ground pepper

Skirt steaks 2, about 4 lb
(2 kg) total weight, trimmed

Flour tortillas 8 large

Fresh cilantro (fresh coriander) ¼ cup (⅓ oz/10 g) minced

Guacamole 2 cups (1 lb/500 g)

Lettuce 1 head, shredded

Fresh salsa and pico de gallo
1 cup (8 oz/250 g) *each*

Monterey jack cheese 1½ cups
(6 oz/185 g) shredded

Crema or sour cream ½ cup
(4 oz/125 g)

Skirt steak is the best choice for quick marinating and grilling. It is well marbled, which makes it very flavorful, and slightly stringy, which makes it chewy—so be sure to slice it across the grain.

To make a marinade, in a bowl, whisk together the oil, onion, garlic, vinegar, chile powder, cumin, and 1 teaspoon pepper.

Cut each steak crosswise into 3 or 4 pieces. There will be thicker pieces and thinner end pieces. Place the meat in a disposable aluminum roasting pan and generously season with salt. Pour the marinade over the meat and turn to coat well. Let stand for 5–10 minutes. Alternatively, dip the steaks in the marinade just before grilling.

Prepare a **CHARCOAL** or **GAS** grill for **DIRECT** grilling over **HIGH** heat (pages 15–16). Brush and oil the grill grate.

Remove the steaks from the marinade and pat dry with paper towels; discard the marinade.

Grill the skirt steak directly over high heat until cooked to your liking, turning once, 3–4 minutes on each side for medium-rare. Wrap the tortillas in aluminum foil and place them on the side of the grill to warm.

Transfer the meat to a carving board, tent with aluminum foil, and let rest for 5 minutes. Slice the steaks across the grain into strips, toss with any accumulated juices from the carving board, and mound onto a platter. Garnish with the cilantro and serve at once with the tortillas, guacamole, lettuce, fresh salsa, pico de gallo, Monterey jack, and crema in separate dishes alongside.

KOREAN-STYLE BARBECUE SHORT RIBS

The national dish of Korea, kalbi kui *are delicious marinated short ribs, usually cooked on a very hot tabletop charcoal grill, sliced, and wrapped in lettuce leaves. Keep a close eye on the grill and be careful not to burn the ribs—they cook very quickly.*

In a dry pan over medium-low heat, toast the sesame seeds just until golden, 1–2 minutes. Set aside. Peel, core, and quarter the pear. To make a marinade, in a blender or food processor, combine the sesame seeds, pear, garlic, green onions, soy sauce, sherry, mirin, sesame oil, brown sugar, and honey. Process on high speed until smooth.

Place the ribs, bone side down, on a cutting board. Using a sharp knife, cut the meat away from the bones; discard or reserve the bones for the marinade. Working with the blade parallel to the cutting board, butterfly each piece of rib meat by cutting three-fourths of the way through and opening it to form a rectangle. Season the meat with salt and pepper and place in a shallow dish with the bones, if using. Pour the marinade over the meat and turn to coat well. Cover and refrigerate for at least 2 hours or up to 4 hours. Remove from the refrigerator 30 minutes before grilling.

Prepare a **CHARCOAL** or **GAS** grill for **DIRECT** grilling over **MEDIUM-HIGH** heat (pages 15–16). Brush and oil the grill grate.

Grill the short ribs directly over medium-high heat, turning once, until browned, caramelized, and cooked to your liking, 6–10 minutes per side for medium-rare.

Transfer the meat to a carving board. Slice the meat and arrange on a platter with the lettuce leaves (using only the outer leaves) and garnish with the cilantro and sliced peppers. Serve hot with the Asian dipping sauce.

Asian Dipping Sauce (page 236)

Sesame seeds 2 tablespoons

Asian pear 1

Garlic 3 cloves

Green (spring) onions 2

Soy sauce and dry sherry ½ cup (4 fl oz/125 ml) *each*

Mirin and Asian dark sesame oil 2 tablespoons *each*

Light brown sugar 1 tablespoon, firmly packed

Honey 1 tablespoon

Beef short ribs 6, about 2 lb (1 kg) total weight, each 2–3 inches (5–7.5 cm) long

Salt and ground pepper

Romaine (cos) lettuce 2 heads

Fresh cilantro (fresh coriander) ¼ cup (⅓ oz/10 g) minced

Chile peppers sliced, for garnish

BISTECCA ALLA FIORENTINA

Florentine-style steak—a T-bone steak grilled over hot coals in a fireplace or wood-burning oven—is one of the jewels of Tuscan cooking. In Italy, bistecca *comes from the Chianina steer, but dry-aged USDA prime or choice beef will duplicate this classic.*

To make an herbed oil, in a small bowl, stir together the oil and herbs.

Trim off the excess fat from the steaks; reserve a 1-inch (2.5-cm) piece to grease the grill grate. Generously season the steaks with salt and pepper, gently pressing it into the meat. Place the steaks in a large baking dish, pour half of the herbed oil over the top, and turn to coat. Cover with plastic wrap and let stand at room temperature for 15 minutes or refrigerate for at least 1 hour or up to 3 hours, turning every hour. Remove from the refrigerator 20 minutes before grilling.

Prepare a **CHARCOAL** or **GAS** grill for **DIRECT** grilling over **MEDIUM-HIGH** heat (pages 15–16). Using tongs, grease the preheated grill grate with the reserved fat; it should smoke and sizzle immediately and begin to melt.

Grill the steaks directly over medium-high heat, turning them occasionally and moving them to a cooler part of the grill if flare-ups occur, 10–12 minutes total or until cooked to your liking.

Transfer the steaks to a carving board, tent with aluminum foil, and let rest for 5 minutes.

Cut the meat from each steak away off the bone in whole pieces and cut each piece into slices ¾ inch (2 cm) thick. Transfer the meat to a serving platter and season with salt, drizzle with the remaining herbed oil, and serve at once.

Olive oil ½ cup (4 fl oz/ 125 ml)

Fresh herbs such as rosemary, sage, thyme, and marjoram 6 tablespoons chopped

T-bone or porterhouse steaks 2, each about 1½–2 lb (750 g–1 kg) and 2 inches (5 cm) thick

Sea salt and cracked pepper

SICILIAN HERB-CRUSTED TRI-TIP

Olive oil 1 cup (8 fl oz/ 250 ml)

Fresh marjoram 2 tablespoons or 1 tablespoon dried oregano

Fresh rosemary 2 tablespoons or 1 tablespoon dried rosemary

Fresh thyme 2 tablespoons or 1 tablespoon dried thyme

Garlic 3 cloves, minced

Yellow onion 1, minced

Cracked pepper 2 tablespoons

Red pepper flakes 1 teaspoon

Tri-tip roast 1, 2½–3 lb (1.25–1.5 kg)

Sea salt

For special occasions, Sicilians rub beef roasts with fresh herbs from the countryside, garlic, and red pepper flakes for extra heat. Fresh herbs work best here, but dried herbs can be substituted.

To make a traditional marinade known as *olio santo,* in a large bowl, stir together the oil, marjoram, rosemary, thyme, garlic, onion, black pepper, and red pepper flakes. Spoon half of the *olio santo* into a small serving bowl and set aside.

Rinse the roast under cold running water and pat dry with paper towels. Place the roast in the large bowl with the remaining *olio santo* and turn to coat well. Cover and let stand at room temperature for 30 minutes, turning once, or refrigerate for at least 1 hour or up to 3 hours, turning every hour to coat. Remove from the refrigerator 30 minutes before grilling.

Prepare a **CHARCOAL** or **GAS** grill for **INDIRECT** grilling over **MEDIUM-HIGH** heat (pages 15–16). Brush and oil the grill grate.

Grill the roast directly over medium-high heat until well marked and charred on the first side, 4–5 minutes. Turn the roast over and cook until charred, about 3 minutes. Move the roast to indirect heat. Spoon any remaining solids left in the marinade over the roast. Cover and grill until the meat is very well charred, crusted, and cooked to your liking, 15–20 minutes longer.

Transfer the roast to a carving board, tent with aluminum foil, and let rest for 5 minutes.

Thinly slice the roast across the grain and lightly season with salt. Serve at once with the reserved *olio santo.*

CHURRASCO-STYLE STEAK WITH CHIMICHURRI

Fresh flat-leaf (Italian) parsley 1 cup (1 oz/30 g)

Fresh cilantro (fresh coriander) 1 cup (1 oz/30 g)

Fresh marjoram 3 tablespoons

Garlic 4 cloves

Sea salt and cracked pepper

Champagne vinegar 3 tablespoons

Olive oil ½ cup (4 fl oz/125 ml)

Red bell pepper (capsicum) ½, roasted, peeled, seeded, and finely diced

Red pepper flakes 1 tablespoon (optional)

Sirloin strip steaks 3, each about ½ lb (250 g) and 1 inch (2.5 cm) thick

Chimichurri is a ubiquitous condiment in Argentina. With its bright acidity and bracing garlic and herb flavor, it enlivens and adds flair to churrasco, *or South American–style grilled meats.*

To make chimichurri, in a food processor, combine the parsley, cilantro, marjoram, and garlic and pulse several times to combine. Scrape down the sides of the bowl and generously season with salt and pepper. Add the vinegar and pulse to incorporate. With the motor running, add the oil in a slow, steady stream until emulsified. Pour into a small serving bowl. Stir in the roasted bell pepper and red pepper flakes, if using. Cover tightly and refrigerate for at least 1 hour or up to overnight. Remove from the refrigerator 20 minutes before grilling.

Trim off the excess fat from the steaks; reserve a 1-inch (2.5-cm) piece to grease the grill grate. Generously season the steaks with salt and cracked pepper and brush with oil.

Prepare a **CHARCOAL** or **GAS** grill for **DIRECT** grilling over **HIGH** heat (pages 15–16). Using tongs, grease the preheated grill grate with the reserved fat; it should smoke and sizzle immediately and begin to melt.

Grill the steaks directly over high heat, turning once, until nicely charred and cooked to your liking, 4–6 minutes per side for medium rare.

Transfer to a carving board, tent with aluminum foil, and let rest for 5 minutes. Slice the steaks across the grain and arrange on a platter. Pour any accumulated juices from the carving board over the top and serve the steaks with the chimichurri drizzled on top.

TEXAS-STYLE BARBECUED BRISKET

In Texas, barbecue means beef, and brisket is king. Here, the brisket is given a spice rub and is slow-smoked over mesquite. Have extra coals or a back-up tank ready because the cooking time is long.

To make a rub, combine the salt, pepper, sugar, paprika, onion powder, garlic, mustard, cumin, and chile powder in a food processor. Process into a coarse powder.

Rinse the brisket under cold running water and pat dry with paper towels. Generously season the brisket all over with the rub, massaging it into the meat. Wrap the brisket in plastic and refrigerate for at least 1 hour or up to overnight. Remove from the refrigerator 30 minutes before grilling.

Prepare a **CHARCOAL** or **GAS** grill for **INDIRECT** grilling over **MEDIUM-LOW** heat (pages 15–16). Brush and oil the grill grate. Unwrap the brisket, season again with the rub, and place it, fat side up, in a large, disposable aluminum roasting pan.

CHARCOAL: Sprinkle half of the soaked wood chips over the coals. Place the roasting pan with the brisket on the grill grate toward side of the grill where the heat is less intense, cover, and grill, basting with any accumulated juices, until mahogany brown in color, 3½–4 hours. Replenish the coals and wood chips every 30 minutes.	**GAS:** Raise a burner to high heat. Heat a smoker box half full of wood chips until smoking; reduce the heat to medium-low. Place the roasting pan with the brisket on the grill grate over the area of lower heat, cover and grill, basting with any accumulated juices, until mahogany brown in color, 3½–4 hours. Replenish the wood chips every 30 minutes.

Transfer the brisket to a large cutting board, tent with aluminum foil, and let rest for 10 minutes. Slice the meat into thin slices. Serve with barbecue sauce on the side and slices of white bread, if using.

Coarse salt ¼ cup (2 oz/60 g)

Ground pepper 3 tablespoons

Light brown sugar 3 tablespoons, firmly packed

Paprika 3 tablespoons

Onion powder 3 tablespoons

Granulated garlic and dry mustard 2 tablespoons *each*

Ground cumin and chile powder 1 tablespoon *each*

Whole beef brisket 1, 5–7 lb (2.5–3.5 kg), trimmed to leave a ¼-inch (6-mm) layer of fat

White bread for serving (optional)

Basic Barbecue Sauce (page 231) for serving (optional)

Mesquite chips 5 lb (2.5 kg), soaked for 30 minutes

THE ULTIMATE GRILLED STEAK

Extra-virgin olive oil
2 tablespoons

Fresh herbs such as rosemary, sage, thyme, and marjoram
3–4 tablespoons chopped

Bone-in rib or boneless rib-eye steaks 2, each 10–12 oz (315–375 g) and 1½–2 inches (4–5 cm) thick

Coarse salt and cracked pepper

Caramelized Onion Jam (page 265) for serving (optional)

The ultimate grilled steak is the holy grail of backyard grillers worldwide. When properly executed, this dish needs no embellishment other than red wine, a green salad, and carnivorous friends with whom to enjoy it. Use your very best olive oil for this simple dish.

In a small bowl, stir together the oil and herbs.

Trim off the excess fat from the steaks; reserve a 1-inch (2.5-cm) piece to grease the grill grate. Generously season the steaks with salt and pepper, gently pressing it into the meat. Place the steaks in a large baking dish, pour the herbed oil over the top, and turn to coat well. Let stand for 10–15 minutes.

Prepare a **CHARCOAL** or **GAS** grill for **DIRECT** grilling over **HIGH** heat (pages 15–16). Using long tongs or a carving fork, grease the preheated grill grate with the reserved fat; it should smoke and sizzle immediately and begin to melt.

Remove the steaks from the marinade, letting the excess drip back into the dish; discard the marinade.

Grill the steaks directly over high heat. Cover and grill until well marked, 2–3 minutes. Turn the steaks, cover, and grill the second sides until grill marks appear. Continue to turn and grill until cooked to your liking.

Transfer the steaks to a carving board, tent with aluminum foil, and let rest for 5 minutes. Cut away the rib bones and thickly slice the steaks. Season with salt and pepper and serve with caramelized onion jam, if using.

SELECTING YOUR STEAK

On or off the bone, the rib steak (or rib-eye) is the first choice of grilling aficionados. The second choice for the ultimate grilled steak is the sirloin strip steak. Look for hormone-free prime or choice rancher's reserve beef, Black Angus, or grass-fed beef. Stay away from pre-packaged select beef displayed in plastic wrap in the supermarket case.

VIETNAMESE FLANK STEAK SALAD

Scoring the meat before marinating it allows the marinade to penetrate and flavor the beef and prevents the steak from curling on the grill. If you can find Thai basil, use it here for authentic flavor.

Spoon one-half of the marinade into a small serving bowl and set aside.

Using a sharp knife, score the meat on both sides in a crosshatch pattern, cutting no more than ½ inch (12 mm) deep. Place the steak in a shallow dish, pour the remaining marinade over the top, and turn to coat well. Cover and refrigerate for at least 1 hour or up to overnight.

Prepare a **CHARCOAL** or **GAS** grill for **DIRECT** grilling over **MEDIUM-HIGH** heat (pages 15–16). Brush and oil the grill grate.

Remove the steak from the marinade, letting the excess drip back into the pan; discard the marinade. Pat the steak dry with paper towels and generously season with salt and pepper.

Grill the steak directly over medium-high heat, turning once and brushing with some of the remaining marinade, until cooked to your liking.

Transfer to a carving board, tent with aluminum foil, and let rest for 5 minutes.

Assemble the salad on individual plates by dividing equal portions of the lettuce, carrot, cucumber, red onion, herbs, and noodles among them. Pour 1 tablespoon of the marinade over the top of each plate.

Slice the steak across the grain into thin strips and place on top of the noodles and salad greens. Garnish with the basil, cilantro, and mint leaves and serve the salad with the remaining marinade alongside.

Spicy Marinade (page 237)

Flank steak 1, 1½–1¾ lb (750–875 g), trimmed

Salt and ground pepper

Bibb (Boston) lettuce 1 head, torn into small pieces

Romaine lettuce 1 head, outer leaves removed, chopped into 1-inch (2.5-cm) chunks

Carrot 1, peeled and julienned

Cucumber 1, peeled, seeded, and julienned

Red onion 1 small, sliced thin

Fresh basil, mint, and cilantro (fresh coriander) leaves 2 tablespoons *each*, minced, plus small leaves for garnish

Dried Asian cellophane noodles 1 lb (500 g), soaked in water until soft, then drained

BACON-WRAPPED FILETS MIGNONS

Filets mignons 6, each 4–5 oz
(125–155 g)

Salt and cracked pepper

Bacon or pancetta
¼ lb (125 g), thinly sliced
(about 12 slices)

Fresh sage leaves 6

Restrained in size and perfectly tender, filets mignons are ideal to grill quickly for a special occasion. Pancetta may be used here, if very thinly sliced. Thick-cut bacon should not be used because it is not on the grill long enough to render its fat and completely cook.

Generously season the filets with salt and pepper, gently pressing it into the meat.

Working with one filet at a time, wrap a bacon slice around the edge of the filet, using a second slice if necessary. Tuck a sage leaf between the bacon and the filet and secure the bacon with a toothpick. Place in a nonaluminum pan, cover, and refrigerate for at least 1 hour or up to 4 hours. Remove from the refrigerator 20 minutes before grilling.

Prepare a **CHARCOAL** or **GAS** grill for **DIRECT** grilling over **MEDIUM-HIGH** heat (pages 15–16). Brush and oil the grill grate.

Grill the filets directly over medium-high heat, turning once, until the beef is well marked and the bacon is crisp, 2–3 minutes per side. Move the filets off direct heat, cover, and finish cooking until done to your liking.

Transfer to a board, tent with aluminum foil, and let rest for 2–3 minutes. Serve.

HEAT ZONES

An experienced grill master knows exactly where the grill is hot and where it's not, and which heat level the food needs. Regardless of the specific grilling method or the type of grill, one section of the grill grate must be searingly hot at all times, with a second zone of lower heat. The art of properly grilling any food lies in the cook's ability to move between heat zones while staying in control of the food and the flame simultaneously. Flare-ups should be avoided. If one should occur, move the food to a cooler part of the grill and let the flame die down. Finished food should be caramelized with distinct grill marks.

BURGERS WITH BLUE CHEESE

The quality of ground beef is of paramount importance; make sure yours comes from a reputable butcher or upscale supermarket. For the best burger, choose well-marbled chuck or sirloin steak with at least 20 percent fat and ask the butcher to grind it twice.

Place the ground beef in a bowl and generously season with salt and pepper. Add 3–4 tablespoons very cold water, as needed, to moisten the meat. Using wet hands, gently work the seasoning and water into the meat, working quickly to keep the meat cool and being careful not to overwork it. Divide the meat into 4 portions. Shape each portion into a patty 3–3½ inches (7.5–9 cm) in diameter and about 1 inch (2.5 cm) thick. Transfer the patties to a platter lined with parchment (baking) or wax paper. Cover and refrigerate for 30 minutes or freeze for 10 minutes.

Prepare a **CHARCOAL** or **GAS** grill for **DIRECT** grilling over **HIGH** heat (pages 15–16). Brush and oil the grill grate.

Brush the hamburger patties with melted butter on both sides and generously season again with salt and pepper.

Grill the burgers directly over high heat until they are well marked and their juices begin to rise to the surface, 2–3 minutes. Turn the burgers over and grill the other side. Move the burgers over indirect heat until cooked to your liking. During the last few minutes of grilling, brush the cut sides of the rolls with the melted butter and grill, cut side down, until lightly toasted, about 1 minute. Turn the rolls and grill for about 30 seconds longer.

Serve the hamburgers on the grilled rolls topped with the blue cheese, lettuce, and the condiments of your choice.

Ground (minced) beef chuck or sirloin 1½ lb (750 g), 75–80% lean

Salt and ground pepper

Unsalted butter 4 tablespoons (2 oz/60 g), melted

Sandwich rolls such as seeded Kaiser 4, split

Blue cheese 4–5 oz (125–155 g), sliced or crumbled

Crisp lettuce leaves such as iceberg or romaine (cos) 1–2 cups (1–2 oz/30–60 g) shredded

Caramelized Onion Jam (page 265), Chipotle Ketchup (page 254), and/or Beer Mustard (page 263) for serving (optional)

BEEF SATAY WITH GINGER DIPPING SAUCE

Ginger Dipping Sauce (page 236)

Soy sauce ½ cup (4 fl oz/ 125 ml)

Asian sesame oil 3 tablespoons

Lemongrass 2 stalks, white parts only, finely diced

Zest and juice of 1 lemon

Garlic 3 cloves, minced

Green (spring) onions 2, white parts only, finely diced

Light brown sugar 2 tablespoons, firmly packed

Flank steak 1, 1½–1¾ lb (750–875 g), trimmed

Salt and ground pepper

Sesame seeds for garnish, toasted (optional)

Bamboo skewers 24

With a little knife work and some skewering skills, grilled beef satays are easy to make, and they are always fun to eat. The lemongrass-scented marinade is a terrific aromatic complement to beefy flank steak, giving it a distinctive Southeast Asian flavor.

Soak the bamboo skewers in water for 30 minutes.

To make a marinade, in a blender or food processor, combine the soy sauce, sesame oil, lemongrass, lemon zest and juice, garlic, green onions, and brown sugar. Process until smooth. Pour into a large measuring cup.

Using a sharp knife, score the meat on both sides in a crosshatch pattern, cutting no more than ¼ inch (16 mm) deep. Slice the meat across the grain on the bias into strips ½ inch (12 mm) thick. One at a time, thread the strips lengthwise onto the skewers. Dip the skewers in the marinade, and then place them in a shallow dish. Cover and refrigerate for at least 1 hour or up to overnight.

Prepare a **CHARCOAL** or **GAS** grill for **DIRECT** grilling over **MEDIUM-HIGH** heat (pages 15–16). Brush and oil the grill grate.

Remove the skewers from the refrigerator and transfer to a plate. Generously season with salt and pepper.

Grill the skewers directly over medium-high heat, turning once, until nicely charred and cooked to your liking, 2–3 minutes per side.

Arrange the skewers on a serving platter, garnish with toasted sesame seeds, and serve at once with the dipping sauce on the side.

CHORIZO WITH CLAMS

Originating in Spain, chorizo is a smoked sausage that is heavily seasoned with paprika and garlic. You can now find it in most butcher shops and upscale supermarkets. The classic paella combination of chorizo and shellfish marries the flavors of smoke and the sea.

Prepare a **CHARCOAL** or **GAS** grill for **DIRECT** grilling over **MEDIUM** heat (pages 15–16). Brush and oil the grill grate.

Prick 4 or 5 very small holes in the casings of the sausages with the tip of a bamboo skewer or toothpick. Grill the sausages directly over medium-high heat, covered, turning frequently to lightly char on all sides, about 12 minutes total. Transfer to a carving board and slice into ½-inch (12-mm) rounds.

Lay out 6 heavy-duty aluminum foil sheets on a work surface. Form the sheets into shallow bowl-shaped packets. Add a handful of clams along with 5 or 6 chorizo slices. Divide the red bell pepper strips, onion, garlic, parsley, and chives. Add a few drops olive oil and 2–3 tablespoons white wine. Season to taste with salt and pepper. Gather the sides of the packets together and fold the top to form a seal.

Roll out a large sheet of heavy-duty aluminum foil and place it on the grill grate. Slide the prepared packets onto the foil sheet and grill the packets over direct heat, covered, until liquid bubbles inside, 5–10 minutes. Move the packets off direct heat. Brush the bread slices with oil and grill over direct heat until lightly charred, about 1 minute per side.

Serve the packets at once for diners to open themselves, being careful of escaping steam. Alternatively, empty the packets into individual serving bowls. Serve the grilled bread alongside.

Chorizo sausages 4 (about 2 lb/1 kg)

Fresh Cherrystone clams or New Zealand cockle clams 2 pints (2 lb/1 kg), rinsed in cold water and scrubbed

Red pepper (capsicum) 1, cored, seeded, and sliced into thin strips

Small onion 1, thinly sliced

Garlic 1 clove, minced

Fresh flat leaf (Italian) parsley 1 cup (1½ oz/45 g) finely chopped

Fresh chives 2 tablespoons finely chopped

Olive oil ½ cup (4 fl oz/ 125 ml)

White wine 1 cup (8 fl oz/ 250 ml)

Salt and ground pepper

Coarse bread ½ loaf, sliced thick

114   BEEF · PORK · LAMB

BEER-BOILED BRATS

Bratwursts 6

Olive oil 2–4 tablespoons, plus oil for brushing

Yellow onion 1 medium, sliced

Pilsner beer 1 bottle (12 fl oz/375 ml), or as needed

Hot dog rolls 6, split

Unsalted butter for brushing melted

Beer Mustard (page 263) and Chipotle Ketchup (page 254) for serving (optional)

Great grilled sausages get even better when bathed in hot beer in a big pot on the grill. First grill the sausages over the fire to pick up smoky flavor from the grill, then simmer them with onions in beer anywhere from 30 minutes to 1 hour. These are perfect for a backyard barbecue or tailgate party.

Prepare a **CHARCOAL** or **GAS** grill for **DIRECT** grilling over **MEDIUM-HIGH** heat (pages 15–16). Brush and oil the grill grate.

Prick the skin of the sausages all over with the tip of a knife. Grill the sausages directly over medium-high heat, turning often, until nicely charred on all sides, 10–15 minutes total. Move the sausages to an area of lower heat. Place a large, heavy pot or Dutch oven over the hottest part of the fire and warm the oil. When the oil is hot, add the onion and cook, stirring often, until soft, 4–5 minutes. Stir in the beer and bring to a boil. Add the grilled sausages, cover, and simmer for at least 30 minutes or up to 1 hour. Add more beer as needed to keep the liquid from boiling away.

During the last few minutes of cooking, brush the inside of the rolls with melted butter and grill directly over the hottest part of the grill, cut side down, until lightly toasted.

Serve the brats in the grilled rolls topped with mustard and ketchup, if using.

CHICAGO-STYLE HOT DOGS

Choose your dogs wisely. All-beef or all-pork hot dogs, or a combination of beef and pork, are the standard. Look for dogs in natural casings, which give the distinctive "snap" and mouthfeel of a properly prepared hot dog.

Prepare a **CHARCOAL** or **GAS** grill for **DIRECT** grilling over **MEDIUM-HIGH** heat (pages 15–16). Brush and oil the grill grate.

Grill the hot dogs directly over medium-high heat, turning often, until lightly charred and plump, about 5 minutes total. Move the hot dogs to indirect heat. Brush the insides of the rolls with melted butter and grill, cut sides down, until lightly toasted, 1 minute. Turn the rolls and grill for about 30 seconds longer.

Serve each hot dog on a roll with equal amounts of the onions, tomato, banana peppers, relish, celery salt, mustard, and a dill pickle spear.

HOT DOG VARIATIONS

New England Ballpark–Style
Grill beef-and-pork hot dogs. Top with chopped grilled onions and peppers, ketchup, mustard, and relish.

New York–Style
Grill beef-and-pork hot dogs on a double thickness of heavy-duty aluminum foil until lightly charred. Top with ketchup, brown mustard, and sauerkraut, if desired. Serve on a warmed white bun accompanied by a fruit smoothie or papaya nectar.

Stuffed Hot Dogs
Halfway through grilling, remove beef-and-pork hot dogs from the grill. Score on the diagonal with incisions ½ inch (12 mm) deep. Insert pickled jalapeño slices into the incisions and top with freshly grated pepper jack cheese. Finish grilling over indirect heat, covered, until the cheese begins to melt. Top with Creole mustard and Chipotle Ketchup (page 254).

Beer Mustard (page 263)

All-beef or beef-and-pork hot dogs 8, preferably with natural casings

Poppy seed hot dog rolls 8, split

Unsalted butter for brushing melted

Yellow onions 1 cup (4 oz/ 125 g) chopped

Tomato 1 cup (6 oz/185 g) chopped

Banana peppers 6, quartered lengthwise

Relish 1 cup (4 oz/125g)

Celery salt

Small dill pickles 2 or 3, quartered lengthwise

BUFFALO BURGERS WITH PEPPER AIOLI

This recipe is an exotic variation on the classic cheeseburger, with a taste of the American Great Plains. A healthier alternative to beef, buffalo meat has a deliciously rich flavor. Because the meat is so lean, take care to avoid overcooking it.

In a large bowl, combine the ground bison, Worcestershire sauce, 3 or 4 dashes of hot-pepper sauce, the granulated garlic, 1½ teaspoons salt, and 1 teaspoon pepper. Using wet hands, gently work the seasoning into the meat, being careful not to overwork it. Divide the meat into 6 equal portions. Shape each portion into a patty 3½ inches (9 cm) in diameter and about 1 inch (2.5 cm) thick. Using your thumb, make a ¾-inch (2-cm) indentation in the center of each patty. Transfer to a plate, cover, and refrigerate for at least 1 hour or up to 4 hours.

Prepare a **CHARCOAL** or **GAS** grill for **DIRECT** grilling over **MEDIUM-HIGH** heat (pages 15–16). Brush and oil the grill grate.

Brush the buffalo burgers with oil on both sides and generously season with salt and pepper. Brush and oil the grill grate.

Grill the burgers directly over medium-high heat until well marked, 2–3 minutes. Turn and grill the burgers until a flavorful crust forms and juices begin to rise to the surface of the patties. Move the burgers to an area of low heat and top with the cheese. Cover and grill until the cheese is melted and the burgers are cooked to your liking, about 2–3 minutes on each side for medium-rare. During the last few minutes of cooking, brush the cut sides of the rolls with the melted butter and grill over the hottest part of the grill, cut sides down, until lightly toasted, about 1 minute. Turn and grill the rolls for about 30 seconds longer.

Serve the burgers on the grilled rolls smeared with pepper aioli and topped with the lettuce and tomatoes. Pass additional pepper aioli at the table.

Pepper Aioli (page 256)

Ground bison meat 1½ lb (750 g)

Worcestershire sauce ¼ cup (2 fl oz/60 ml)

Hot-pepper sauce

Granulated garlic 1 teaspoon

Coarse salt and ground pepper

Olive oil for brushing

Gruyère cheese 6 slices

Unsalted butter for brushing melted

Brioche rolls, Kaiser rolls, or seeded hamburger rolls 6, split

Green leaf lettuce 6–10 leaves, trimmed to fit the rolls

Heirloom tomatoes 2, sliced

120   BEEF · PORK · LAMB

BABY BACK RIBS

Basic Barbecue Sauce (page 231)

Paprika ½ cup (4 oz/125 g)

Granulated garlic ¼ cup (4 oz/125 g)

Light brown sugar 2 tablespoons, firmly packed

Chile powder 1 tablespoon

Dry mustard and ground cumin 1 teaspoon, *each*

Coarse salt 1 tablespoon

Ground pepper 1 teaspoon

Baby back pork ribs 4 slabs, about 5 lb (2.5 kg), trimmed

Mesquite wood chunks or chips 4–5 lb (2–2.25 kg), soaked for 30 minutes

If needed, you can start the ribs in the oven and finish them on the grill. Heat the oven to 350°F (180°C) and roast the ribs in a shallow roasting pan for 2–2½ hours, turning occasionally, until they are cooked through, and then transfer them to the grill for smoky flavor.

To make a dry rub, in a small bowl, stir together the paprika, granulated garlic, brown sugar, chile powder, mustard, cumin, salt, and pepper.

Rinse the ribs under cold running water and pat dry with paper towels. Generously season all over with the rub, massaging it in. Cover and refrigerate overnight.

Prepare a **CHARCOAL** or **GAS** grill for **INDIRECT** grilling over **MEDIUM-LOW** heat (pages 15–16). Brush and oil the grill grate.

CHARCOAL: Rake the coals to the sides of the grill and place a drip pan in the fire bed. Sprinkle half the wood chips over the coals. Grill the ribs, covered, until fork-tender and well browned, 3–3½ hours, replenishing the coals and wood chips every hour to maintain temperature and smoke. Transfer the ribs to a cutting board and cut each slab into 3- or 4-rib portions. To finish, brush with barbecue sauce on both sides and grill over direct heat until cooked through.

GAS: Raise a burner to high heat. Heat a smoker box half full of wood chips until smoking; reduce the heat to medium-low. Grill the ribs, covered, until fork-tender and browned, 3–3½ hours, replenishing the wood chips every hour. Transfer the ribs to a cutting board and cut each slab into 3- or 4-rib portions. To finish, brush with barbecue sauce on both sides and grill over direct heat until cooked through.

Transfer the ribs to a cutting board. Cut the ribs between the bones and pile high on a platter. Serve at once with additional barbecue sauce on the side.

SPIT-ROASTED PIG

To successfully spit-roast a pig, you'll need a hog rotisserie, shovel, steel wire and wire cutters, a heavy-duty trussing needle, butcher's twine, and two pairs of heavy-duty oven mitts. For roasting instructions, see the Pig Roast grilling adventure on pages 45–47.

Prepare a fire pit (page 46) for **INDIRECT** grilling over **MEDIUM-HIGH** heat (pages 15–16).

Rub the inside of the pig and the pork roasts with the chile rub. Thread the spit through the pig. Place the pork roasts inside the belly cavity. Use a heavy-duty trussing needle and butcher's twine to sew the cavity closed. Tie the pig closed with more twine at 6- to 8-inch (15- to 20-cm) intervals. Tie the feet and legs together with butcher's twine and brush all over with oil.

Attach the pig on its spit to the mounting brackets or tripods over indirect heat, 1–2 feet (30–60 cm) above and 1–2 feet (30–60 cm) away from the fire. Secure the spit rod to the brackets with wire. Place 2 large disposable aluminum roasting pans under the pig to catch the drippings. Turn on the motor. Keep an oven thermometer situated on a rock or cinder block near the pig to check the ambient temperature. Add more charcoal and shovel the coals to maintain an ambient temperature of 225–250°F (110–120°C). Roast the pig until the skin is golden brown and crisp and the pig is cooked through to an internal temperature of 155–160°F (68–71°C). This will take 8–10 hours, depending on your fire pit. Take internal temperature readings in the thickest parts of the shoulder and hindquarters. Lightly brush the pig all over with mop sauce occasionally during the roasting time to keep the skin moist and impart flavor.

This next step is a two-man job: Wearing heavy-duty oven mitts, lift the pig on the spit out of the pit and transfer it to a work station or board large enough to accommodate it. Remove the spit rod from the pig, including all wires and butcher's twine used to secure the pig. Carve the pig in sections, starting at the cheeks and shoulder and working your way through the ribs and tenderloin to the hindquarters. Remove the pork butts from the belly cavity and carve them against the grain. Serve at once with barbecue sauce, if using, and other condiments of choice.

Chile Rub (page 245) double recipe

Memphis Mop Sauce (page 232)

Whole pig 1, about 50 lb (25 kg) total weight

Boneless pork butt shoulder roasts (Boston butt) 2, each 6–7 lb (3–4 kg), skin removed, with a thick layer of fat remaining

Olive oil 2 cups (16 fl oz/ 500 ml)

Basic Barbecue Sauce (page 231) for serving (optional)

PORK CHOPS WITH GRILLED APPLE PURÉE

**Grilled Apple Purée
(page 266)**

Light brown sugar 3
tablespoons, firmly packed

Granulated garlic
2 tablespoons or 5 cloves
garlic, crushed into a paste

Bay leaves 2–3

Fresh rosemary 2 tablespoons
minced, plus 4 sprigs for
garnish

Allspice berries 5, or
1 teaspoon ground allspice

Salt and ground pepper
1 teaspoon *each*

**Bone-in or boneless loin pork
chops** 4, each about ¾ inch
(2 cm) thick

Pork chops have a tendency to dry out on the grill, but brining them beforehand is the secret to adding moisture and extra flavor. Many varieties of tart apples are available year-round, and when they are brushed with melted butter and spices and grilled, they become a perfect complement to the pork.

To make the brine, in a medium saucepan over high heat, combine 2 cups (16 fl oz/500 ml) water, the brown sugar, granulated garlic, bay leaves, rosemary, allspice, and 1 teaspoon each salt and pepper. Bring to a boil, stirring to dissolve the sugar, garlic, and salt. Remove from the heat and let cool slightly. Add 2 more cups water, transfer to a large nonaluminum container, and refrigerate until cold, about 1 hour.

Add the pork chops to the cold brine and refrigerate for at least 1 hour.

Remove the pork chops from the brine and pat dry with paper towels; discard the brine. Season the chops on both sides with salt and pepper.

Prepare a **CHARCOAL** or **GAS** grill for **DIRECT** grilling over **MEDIUM-HIGH** heat (pages 15–16). Brush the grill grate with oil.

Grill the pork chops directly over medium-high heat, until nicely grill-marked, about 2 minutes. Turn the pork chops and grill the second sides until well marked and cooked to your liking.

Transfer the grilled pork chops to a serving platter, top with a heaping spoonful of the grilled apple purée, and garnish with the rosemary sprigs.

LEMON-DILL PORK TENDERLOIN

In this recipe, lemon-dill marinade provides a bright complementary flavor to pork tenderloins, which, because of their long narrow shape, cook quickly and are very easy to grill.

To make a lemon-dill marinade, in a shallow dish large enough to accommodate the pork, stir together the olive oil, the zest and juice of 2 of the lemons, dill, and garlic. Add the pork and turn to coat well. Cover and refrigerate, turning occasionally, for at least 1 hour or up to 4 hours.

Prepare a **CHARCOAL** or **GAS** grill for **DIRECT** grilling over **MEDIUM-HIGH** heat (pages 15–16). Brush and oil the grill grate.

Remove the pork from the marinade, letting the excess drip back into the dish, and pat dry; reserve the marinade. Brush the pork with oil and generously season with salt and pepper.

Grill the pork directly over medium-high heat, turning occasionally, until well marked on all sides. Move the tenderloins over indirect heat, cover the grill, and cook until firm to the touch and cooked through, 10–15 minutes longer.

To test for doneness, insert an instant-read thermometer into the thickest part of the loin; it should register 150°F (65°C). The temperature will rise a few more degrees while the meat is resting.

Transfer the pork to a carving board, tent with aluminum foil, and let rest for 5 minutes. While the pork is resting, halve the remaining 2 lemons and place on the grill, cut side down.

Cut pork into slices ¾ inch (2 cm) thick and arrange on a serving platter with the grilled lemons. Garnish with dill fronds and serve at once.

Olive oil ½ cup (4 fl oz/ 125 ml)

Lemons 4

Fresh dill 2 tablespoons roughly chopped, plus fronds for garnish

Garlic 2 cloves, minced

Pork tenderloins 2, about 3 lb (1.5 kg) each, trimmed and tied to make a compact, uniform shape

Salt and ground pepper

GROUND LAMB KEBABS

Mint Raita (page 267) and
Cucumber Relish (page 254)

Garlic 4 cloves

Coarse salt and ground pepper

Yellow onion 1, minced

Fresh bread crumbs ¼ cup
(½ oz/15 g)

Fresh mint ¼ cup (⅓ oz/
10 g) finely chopped

Fresh flat-leaf (Italian) parsley
3 tablespoons finely chopped

Ground cumin 2 teaspoons

Ground coriander 1 teaspoon

Ground cayenne ½ teaspoon

Ground lamb shoulder
2 lb (32 oz/1 kg), 80–85% lean

Olive oil 1 tablespoon

Naan, pita, or lavash 8 pieces

Tomatoes and grilled onions
for serving, finely chopped

Long, flat metal skewers 8

In many parts of the world, street vendors grill spiced ground lamb kebabs and serve them on flatbread for a quick snack on the go. Raita, a South Asian minted yogurt sauce, tastes best the day it is made but can be tightly covered and refrigerated for up to 2 days.

Using the flat side of a chef's knife, crush and smear the garlic into a paste with 1 teaspoon coarse salt. In a large bowl, stir together the garlic paste, onion, bread crumbs, mint, parsley, cumin, coriander, and cayenne. Add the ground lamb and generously season with salt and pepper. Using wet hands, gently work the seasoning into the meat. Divide the mixture into 8 portions.

Coat the bottom of a shallow dish with the oil. Using wet hands, shape each meat portion into a sausage 3–3½ inches (7.5–9 cm) long and 1 inch (2.5 cm) in diameter. Carefully thread each sausage onto a skewer and set aside. Roll the kebabs in the oil to coat and arrange them in the dish. Cover and refrigerate for at least 1 hour or up to 4 hours. Remove the skewers from the refrigerator 10 minutes before grilling.

Prepare a **CHARCOAL** or **GAS** grill for **DIRECT** grilling over **HIGH** heat (pages 15–16). Brush and oil the grill grate.

Grill the kebabs directly over high heat, turning often, until nicely charred on all sides and cooked through, 8–10 minutes total. Place the naan, pita or lavash over indirect heat and grill until warm, about 2 minutes.

Transfer the kebabs and grilled flatbread to a platter. Serve with the raita, cucumber relish, tomatoes, and grilled onions.

VEAL CHOPS IN HERBED MARINADE

Wood-grilled veal chops are perfect fare for special occasions. Here the delicate flavor of the veal is enhanced with a marinade of olive oil and Mediterranean herbs, then finished with a silky demi-glace.

To make a rosemary demi-glace, in a small saucepan over high heat, combine the wine and 1 cup (8 fl oz/250 ml) water and bring to a boil. Remove from the heat and whisk in the demi-glace until smooth. Place the saucepan over low heat, add the 3 sprigs each rosemary and thyme, and simmer until reduced slightly, 10–15 minutes. Strain through a sieve into another small saucepan; discard the herbs. Keep the demi-glace warm on the stove top.

In a small bowl, stir together the oil and the chopped rosemary and thyme. Place the veal chops in a shallow dish and generously season with salt and pepper. Pour the herbed oil over the meat and turn to coat well. Cover and let stand for 10–15 minutes.

Prepare a **CHARCOAL** or **GAS** grill for **DIRECT** grilling over **MEDIUM-HIGH** heat (pages 15–16). Brush and oil the grill grate.

Grill the veal chops directly over medium-high heat, turning once, until well marked and charred, 4–6 minutes per side. Move the chops to indirect heat, cover, and grill until firm to the touch and cooked to your liking.

Transfer the chops to a large serving platter, tent with aluminum foil, and let rest for 5 minutes.

Rewarm the demi-glace if needed. Add the butter cubes to the demi-glace, one at a time, whisking after each addition. Strain any accumulated meat juices into the demi-glace.

Garnish the chops with rosemary and thyme sprigs and spoon sauce over the chops, or pass the chops at the table with the sauce on the side.

Red wine 1 cup (8 fl oz/ 250 ml)

Veal demi-glace ¼ cup (2 fl oz/60 ml)

Fresh rosemary 3 sprigs plus 2 tablespoons roughly chopped, plus more sprigs for garnish

Fresh thyme 3 sprigs plus 2 tablespoons roughly chopped, plus more sprigs for garnish

Olive oil ¼ cup (2 fl oz/60 ml)

Veal chops 6, each 1 inch (2.5 cm) thick

Salt and ground pepper

Unsalted butter 1–2 tablespoons cold, cubed

128   BEEF • PORK • LAMB

MOROCCAN-SPICED RACK OF LAMB

Herbed Couscous (page 267)

Garlic 3 cloves

Salt and cracked pepper

Olive oil ½ cup (4 fl oz/ 125 ml)

Unsalted butter ½ cup (4 oz/125 g)

Shallot 1 medium, minced

Zest and juice of 1 lemon

Fresh mint ½ cup (¾ oz/ 20 g) minced, plus leaves for garnish

Fresh thyme 1 tablespoon minced or 2 teaspoons dried thyme

Ground cumin and ground coriander 1 teaspoon *each*

Racks of lamb 2, 1¼–1½ lb (625–750 g) each, cut into 2–3 rib portions

Tender and flavorful rack of lamb—rib bones with the tenderloin attached—shouldn't be restricted to holiday fare or fancy restaurant menus. Simply dressed with herbs or marinated briefly to add moisture and flavor, grilled rack of lamb makes any occasion special.

Using the flat side of a chef's knife, crush and smear the garlic into a paste with 1 teaspoon salt. To make a spiced butter, in a small saucepan over medium heat, warm the oil and melt the butter until the foam subsides. Stir in the garlic paste, shallot, lemon zest and juice, mint, thyme, cumin, and coriander. Reduce the heat to medium-low and cook for 3–4 minutes. Let cool slightly.

Prepare a **CHARCOAL** or **GAS** grill for **DIRECT** grilling over **MEDIUM-HIGH** heat (pages 15–16). Brush and oil the grill grate.

Generously season the lamb with salt and pepper and brush with the spiced butter. Tightly wrap the ends of the lamb bones in heavy-duty aluminum foil to prevent them from scorching during grilling.

Grill the lamb directly over medium-high heat until well marked on all sides. Transfer the lamb rack to indirect heat, cover the grill, and cook until firm to the touch, 10–12 minutes, or until cooked to your liking.

To serve, slice the lamb racks between the bones into individual chops. Arrange the chops on top of the couscous. Drizzle with any remaining spiced butter and garnish with mint leaves.

Poultry

CLASSIC BARBECUED CHICKEN

This recipe highlights the distinction between grilling and barbecuing. For added flavor, use fresh rosemary sprigs in place of a basting brush to apply the barbecue sauce onto the chicken.

Rinse the chickens under cold running water and pat dry. Generously season with the chile rub. Carefully loosen the skin from the breast and the legs with your fingers and massage the rub under the skin. Cover and refrigerate for 1 hour or up to overnight. Remove from the refrigerator 20 minutes before grilling.

Prepare a **CHARCOAL** or **GAS** grill for **INDIRECT** grilling over **MEDIUM-LOW** heat (pages 15–16). Brush and oil the grill grate.

Chile Rub (page 245)

Basic Barbecue Sauce (page 231) or Molasses Barbecue Sauce (page 231) ²/₃ cup (5 fl oz/160 ml), plus more for serving

Fryer chickens 2, each about 3½ lb (1.75 kg), neck, giblets, and wing tips removed, split in half

Rosemary sprigs for brushing the chicken (optional)

Wood chips or chunks such as mesquite, hickory, or applewood 1–3 lb (500 g–1.5 kg), soaked for 30 minutes

CHARCOAL: Rake the coals to the sides of the grill and place a drip pan with ½ inch (12 mm) water in the fire bed. Sprinkle half the wood chips over the coals. Place the chicken on the grate over the pan, cover, and cook until the juices run clear when the thigh is pierced, 60–75 minutes. Replenish the coals and wood chips every 15 minutes to maintain constant temperature and smoke. Remove the pan and rake the coals to the center. Move the chicken over the coals. Brush with the barbecue sauce and grill until caramelized.

GAS: Raise a burner to high. Heat a smoker box half full of wood chips until smoking; reduce heat to medium-low. Place a drip pan with ½ inch (12 mm) water over the heating elements. Place the chicken on the grate over the drip pan, cover, and cook until the juices run clear when the thigh is pierced, 60–75 minutes. Replenish the chips every 15 minutes to maintain constant smoke. Remove the pan. Move the chicken over the heating elements. Brush with the barbecue sauce and grill until caramelized.

Transfer chicken to a cutting board, tent with aluminum foil, and let rest for 10 minutes. Transfer to a platter and serve at once with barbecue sauce on the side.

PULLED BARBECUED CHICKEN

Pulled barbecued chicken can be used as an ingredient in sandwiches, quesadillas, or even chicken salad. After smoke-grilling the whole bird, pull the meat from the bones and dress with barbecue sauce.

Rinse the chicken, inside and out, under cold running water and pat dry. Season, inside and out, with salt and pepper. Carefully loosen the skin from the breast and the legs with your fingers. Rub the chile rub under the skin and all over the outside of the chickens. Stuff the onion and herb sprigs into the cavity. Truss the chicken and place in a disposable aluminum roasting pan. Cover and refrigerate for at least 1 hour or up to overnight. Remove from the refrigerator 20 minutes before grilling.

Prepare a **CHARCOAL** or **GAS** grill for **INDIRECT** grilling over **MEDIUM-LOW** heat (pages 15–16). Brush and oil the grill grate.

CHARCOAL: Rake the coals to the sides of the grill and place a drip pan with ½ inch (12 mm) water in the fire bed. Sprinkle half of the wood chips over the coals. Place the pan with the chicken on the grate, cover, and cook until the juices run clear when the thigh is pierced, 1¼–1½ hours. Replenish the coals and chips every 15 minutes to maintain constant temperature and smoke; add more water to the drip pan, if needed.

GAS: Raise a burner to high. Heat a smoker box half full of wood chips until smoking; reduce heat to medium-low. Place a drip pan with ½ inch (12 mm) water over the heating elements. Place the pan with the chicken on the grate over the pan, cover, and cook until the juices run clear when the thigh is pierced, 1¼–1½ hours. Replenish the chips every 30 minutes to maintain constant smoke; add more water to the drip pan, if needed.

Insert an instant-read thermometer into the thickest part of the thigh away from the bone; it should register 170°F (77°C). Transfer the chicken to a carving board, tent with foil, and let rest for 10 minutes before pulling the meat from the bones.

Chile Rub (page 245)

Basic Barbecue Sauce (page 231)

Chicken 1, 3½–4 lb (1.75–2 kg), neck, giblets, and wing tips removed

Salt and pepper

Yellow onion 1, quartered

Fresh herbs such as rosemary, sage, and/or thyme 5–10 sprigs

Hardwood chips or chunks 1–3 lb (500–1500 g), soaked for 30 minutes

JERK CHICKEN WITH STONE FRUIT CHUTNEY

Jerk Marinade (page 241)

Stone Fruit Chutney (page 265)

Chicken legs and thighs 6

Tomato ketchup ¼ cup (2 oz/60 g)

Soy sauce 2 tablespoons

Malt vinegar 3 tablespoons

Fruitwood chips or chunks 1–2 lb (500 g–1 kg), soaked for 30 minutes

The sweet, sour, fiery marinade of this Jamaican chicken also serves as the base for a basting sauce to use during grilling. Overnight marinating guarantees that the flavors penetrate the meat.

Rinse the chicken under cold running water and pat dry. Arrange the chicken in a single layer in a nonaluminum roasting pan. Pour two-thirds of the jerk marinade over the chicken and turn to coat. Reserve the remaining marinade. Cover and refrigerate for up to 4–5 hours or overnight, turning occasionally.

To make a barbecue sauce, mix together the remaining marinade, ketchup, soy sauce, and vinegar and set aside until ready to use.

Prepare a **CHARCOAL** or **GAS** grill for **INDIRECT** grilling over **MEDIUM** heat (pages 15–16). Brush and oil the grill grate.

CHARCOAL: Rake the coals to the sides of the grill and place a drip pan with ½ inch (12 mm) water in the fire bed. Sprinkle a third of the wood chips over the coals. Place the chicken on the grate over the pan. Cover and cook, turning once, until browned, 20–30 minutes. Remove the pan and rake the coals to the center of the grill. Place the chicken directly over the coals and brush with the barbecue sauce. Grill, turning and basting often, until charred on all sides, 5–10 minutes longer.

GAS: Raise a burner to high. Heat a smoker box half full of wood chips until smoking; reduce heat to medium-low. Place a drip pan with ½ inch (12 mm) water over the heating elements. Place the chicken on the grate over the drip pan. Cover and cook, turning once, until browned on all sides, 20–30 minutes. Remove the pan. Move the chicken to grill directly over medium heat and brush with the barbecue sauce. Grill, turning and basting often, until nicely charred on all sides, 5–10 minutes longer.

Transfer to a platter and serve at once with the stone fruit chutney on the side.

CHICKEN THIGHS DIAVOLO

Cider vinegar ¼ cup
(2 fl oz/60 ml)

Paprika 2 tablespoons

**Cayenne pepper and
granulated garlic**
1 tablespoon *each*

Coarse salt 1 tablespoon

Cracked pepper 1 tablespoon

Chile powder 2 teaspoons

**Thai chile paste or red pepper
flakes** 1 teaspoon

Hot-pepper sauce 1 teaspoon

Bone-in chicken thighs
3 lb (1.5 kg) or 2 lb (1 kg)
boneless chicken thigh meat

Wood chips 1 or 2 handfuls,
soaked for 30 minutes

*Seasoned with five different chile spices, these spicy chicken thighs
are highly addictive. Though not as popular as chicken breasts, juicy
thigh meat is considered by many to be the tastiest part of the bird.*

In a nonaluminum bowl, make a sauce by combining the vinegar, paprika, cayenne,
granulated garlic, salt, pepper, chile powder, chile paste, and hot-pepper sauce.
Add ½ cup (4 fl oz/125 ml) water and whisk vigorously until the salt and granulated
garlic dissolve. Taste and adjust the seasoning; the sauce should be bright red and
very spicy. Pour half the sauce into a small serving bowl and set aside.

Rinse the chicken under cold running water and pat dry. Using a sharp knife, score
the chicken to the bone in several places to expose the flesh. Place the chicken in
a large disposable aluminum roasting pan, pour the remaining sauce over the top,
and turn to coat well. Cover and marinate in the refrigerator for at least 1 hour
or up to 4 hours. Remove from the refrigerator 10 minutes before grilling.

Prepare a **CHARCOAL** or **GAS** grill for **INDIRECT** grilling over **MEDIUM** heat
(pages 15–16). Remove the chicken from the marinade, reserving the marinade.

CHARCOAL: Sprinkle the wood
chips over the coals. Place the pan
with the thighs on the cooler side
of the grill, cover, and cook until
cooked through, about 30 minutes.
Transfer the thighs to the grate
directly over the coals, brush with
the marinade from the pan, and
grill, turning often, until nicely
charred on all sides, about
3–5 minutes more.

GAS: Raise a burner to high. Heat
a smoker box half full of chips until
smoking; reduce heat to medium-
low. Place the pan with the thighs
over unlit burners, cover, and cook
until cooked through, 30 minutes.
Transfer the thighs to the grate
directly over the heat, brush with
the marinade from the pan, and
grill, turning often, until nicely
charred, 3–5 minutes more.

Transfer to a platter and serve at once with the reserved sauce on the side.

JALAPEÑO STICKY WINGS

These spicy wings are an addictive starter, so be prepared to make a second—or third—batch right away. Kids of all ages will go crazy for these. Wash them down with Sparkling Mint Lemonade (page 218) or Spiked Arnold Palmers (page 225).

Preheat a broiler (grill) on high. Line a baking sheet with aluminum foil.

In a small saucepan over medium heat, melt the butter. Stir in the jalapeño jelly, honey, chiles, granulated garlic, paprika, chile powder, cayenne, and a pinch each of salt and pepper. Keep warm on the stove top.

Rinse the chicken wings under cold running water and pat dry with paper towels. Working in batches, arrange the wings on a single layer on the baking sheet. Broil, turning once, until lightly browned and cooked through, 10–15 minutes.

Prepare a **CHARCOAL** or **GAS** grill for **DIRECT** grilling over **MEDIUM-HIGH** heat (pages 15–16). Brush and oil the grill grate.

Grill the wings directly over medium-high heat, turning occasionally, until charred with grill marks on all sides, 4–5 minutes.

In a large bowl, combine the chicken wings and the jalapeño mixture and toss to coat. Transfer to a serving plate and serve at once.

Unsalted butter 4 tablespoons (2 oz/60 g)

Jalapeño or pepper jelly ¼ cup (2½ oz/75 g)

Honey or light agave syrup 2 tablespoons

Jalapeño chiles 2, seeded and finely chopped, or 1 can (4 oz/125 g) fire-roasted jalapeño chiles, drained and finely diced

Granulated garlic 1 teaspoon

Paprika ½ teaspoon

Chile powder ½ teaspoon

Cayenne pepper ½ teaspoon

Coarse salt and ground pepper

Chicken wings 3 lb (1.5 kg), about 30, cut at the joints, wing tips discarded

BLACK PEPPER CHICKEN WINGS

Chicken wings are one of the most perfect finger foods to ever grace a grill: They're fun to eat and easy to prepare, and they take to a vast array of spices and sauces. For spur-of-the-moment entertaining, keep a supply of frozen wings on hand in your freezer—just increase the cooking time by 10 minutes.

Position a rack 4 inches (10 cm) from the broiler (grill) and preheat the broiler on high. Line a baking sheet with heavy-duty aluminum foil and lightly brush with oil.

Rinse the chicken wings under cold running water and pat dry with paper towels. Arrange the wings in a single layer on the prepared baking sheet and season generously with salt and pepper. Broil, turning once, until lightly browned and cooked through, about 15 minutes total. Let the wings cool slightly on the pan.

In a bowl, combine the mayonnaise and buttermilk. Stir in 1 teaspoon salt, 1 tablespoon pepper, and a few dashes of hot-pepper sauce. Add the wings and toss to coat.

Prepare a **CHARCOAL** or **GAS** grill for **DIRECT** grilling over **MEDIUM-HIGH** heat (pages 15–16). Brush and oil the grill grate.

Working in batches as needed to prevent crowding, grill the wings directly over medium-high heat, turning once, until the skin is lightly charred and crispy, 4–5 minutes per side. Move the wings to the edge of the grill where the heat is less intense, baste with some of the barbecue sauce or glaze, and grill until tender, 15–20 minutes.

Transfer the wings to a platter and serve at once with remaining barbecue sauce or glaze.

Vegetable oil for brushing

Chicken wings about 24 pieces, 2–2½ lb (1–1.25 kg), cut at the joints, wing tips discarded

Coarse salt and cracked pepper

Mayonnaise ¼ cup (2 fl oz/ 60 ml)

Buttermilk ¼ cup (2 fl oz/ 60 ml)

Hot-pepper sauce

Basic Barbecue Sauce (page 231), Mustard Glaze (page 246), Soy Glaze (page 248), or Spicy Honey Glaze (page 246) 1 cup (8 fl oz/250 ml)

CHICKEN BREAST SPIEDINI

Basil-Green Garlic Dipping Sauce (page 237)

Olive oil ¼ cup (2 fl oz/ 60 ml)

Fresh rosemary and oregano or marjoram 1 tablespoon *each,* roughly chopped

Coarse salt and ground pepper

Skinless, boneless roaster chicken breast 2½ lb (1.25 kg)

Pinot grigio or other dry white wine ¼ cup (2 fl oz/60 ml)

Onion 1, cut into 1-inch (2.5-cm) chunks

Red bell pepper and green bell pepper (capsicum) 1 *each,* seeded and cut into 1-inch (2.5-cm) chunks

Red cherry tomatoes 8

Long, flat metal skewers 8

These are chicken and vegetable skewers, Italian-style. The dipping sauce tastes best within 1 hour of making it, but it can be tightly covered and refrigerated for up to 2 days.

To make an herbed oil, in a small bowl, stir together the oil, rosemary, oregano, 1 teaspoon salt, and 1 teaspoon pepper. Set aside.

Rinse the chicken, inside and out, under cold running water and pat dry with paper towels. Using a sharp boning knife, cut the tenderloins from each side of the chicken breast and cut them in half crosswise. Cut the chicken on the bias into slices ½ inch (12 mm) thick. Place the chicken in a nonaluminum bowl and season with salt and pepper. Add the wine and half of the herbed oil and turn to coat. Cover and let stand at room temperature for 10–15 minutes or refrigerate for 1–4 hours. Remove from the refrigerator 20 minutes before grilling.

To assemble, thread the chicken slices and onion and bell pepper chunks onto the skewers, alternating between them (each skewer should have 4 chicken slices). Thread a cherry tomato onto the end of each skewer.

Prepare a **CHARCOAL** or **GAS** grill for **DIRECT** grilling over **MEDIUM-HIGH** heat (pages 15–16). Brush and oil the grill grate.

Grill the skewers directly over medium-high heat, turning often and brushing with the reserved herbed oil, until the chicken is cooked through and the vegetables are nicely charred, 8–12 minutes total.

Transfer the spiedini to individual plates or a large platter and drizzle with the basil-green garlic dipping sauce. Serve at once.

CHICKEN YAKITORI WITH HONEY SAUCE

HONEY SAUCE

Soy sauce ½ cup (4 fl oz/ 125 ml)

Mirin or other rice wine ¼ cup (2 fl oz/60 ml)

Sake ¼ cup (2 fl oz/60 ml)

Honey 3 tablespoons

Garlic 2 cloves, minced

Fresh ginger 2 tablespoons peeled and grated

Green (spring) onions 2, white and green parts, finely chopped

Iceberg lettuce ½ head, cored and shredded (optional)

Skinless, boneless chicken thighs 2½ lb (1.25 kg)

Salt

Sesame oil for brushing

Bamboo skewers 24

Japanese culinary tradition is filled with delicious grilled meats, fish, poultry, and vegetable dishes. Chicken yakitori is Japanese grilling simplicity at its best. Small amounts of skewered thigh meat, cooked quickly over very hot coals, is served with a dipping sauce.

Soak the bamboo skewers in water for 30 minutes.

To make the honey sauce, in a small saucepan over high heat, combine the soy sauce, mirin, sake, honey, garlic, ginger, and green onions and bring to a boil. Reduce the heat to medium and simmer until slightly thickened and glossy, about 10 minutes. Strain into a bowl, cover, and refrigerate until ready to use.

Mound the lettuce, if using, in the center of a serving platter; set aside.

Rinse the chicken under cold running water and pat dry with paper towels. Using a sharp knife, cut each thigh into three strips, each about 2 inches (5 cm) long and ½ inch (12 mm) thick. Thread 3 or 4 chicken pieces onto each soaked skewer without crowding. Lightly season the skewers with salt and brush lightly with oil.

Prepare a **CHARCOAL** or **GAS** grill for **DIRECT** grilling over **HIGH** heat (pages 15–16). Brush and oil the grill grate.

Grill the skewers directly over high heat, turning once, until well marked and cooked through, 3–4 minutes per side.

Arrange the skewers on top of the lettuce, if using, on the platter. Drizzle some of the honey sauce on top. Serve at once with the remaining sauce on the side.

CHICKEN UNDER A BRICK

Grilling a butterflied chicken under a brick is a great way to get crispy skin every time. The brick weighs down the chicken, ensuring good grill marks. If you don't have a brick, use a heavy-cast iron pan.

In a dry frying pan over medium heat, toast the fennel seeds and peppercorns until fragrant, 3–4 minutes. Transfer to a plate and let cool completely. Pour the spices into a spice grinder or blender and process into a coarse powder.

Using a microplane grater, grate the zest from the lemon; halve the fruit and reserve. In a small bowl, stir together the lemon zest, toasted spice mixture, sage, thyme, granulated garlic, chile powder, and 1 tablespoon salt.

Rinse the chicken under cold running water and pat dry with paper towels. Place the chicken in a large roasting pan. Rub the chicken all over with the spice-herb mixture; reserve any extra rub to season the chicken again right before grilling. Cover and refrigerate for at least 1 hour or up to overnight. Remove from the refrigerator 30 minutes before grilling and pat dry with paper towels.

Prepare a **CHARCOAL** or **GAS** grill for **INDIRECT** grilling over **MEDIUM-HIGH** heat (pages 15–16). Wrap a brick in two sheets of heavy-duty aluminum foil and preheat over the hottest part of the fire. Brush and oil the grill grate.

Squeeze 1 of the reserved lemon halves over the chicken and brush with oil. Season the chicken with any remaining spice-herb mixture.

Place the chicken, skin side down, on the cooler side of the grill. Place the brick on top of the chicken, cover, and cook until chicken is grill marked, 8–10 minutes. Remove the brick and move the chicken, still skin side down, directly over the hottest part of the fire. Replace the brick, cover, and cook until nicely charred, 10–12 minutes. Turn the chicken over, replace the brick, and grill until the juices run clear when the thickest part of the thigh is pierced, 15–20 minutes longer.

Transfer the bird to a carving board, tent with aluminum foil, and let rest for 5–10 minutes before carving and serving.

Fennel seeds 1 tablespoon

White peppercorns 1 tablespoon

Lemon 1

Fresh sage 2 tablespoons finely chopped or 1 tablespoon dried sage

Fresh thyme 1 tablespoon roughly chopped or 2 teaspoons dried thyme

Granulated garlic 1 tablespoon

Chile powder ½ teaspoon

Coarse salt

Young chicken 1, 3½–4 lb (1.75–2 kg), neck, giblets, and wing tips removed, butterflied

Olive oil or duck fat for brushing

BUTTERMILK-BRINED CHICKEN

Chicken breasts are notorious for drying out on the grill, but here a buttermilk brine comes to the rescue. The acidic buttermilk acts as a tenderizer to help the chicken breasts stay moist. Serve with Grilled Fingerling Potatoes (page 204) or Panzanella Salad (page 87).

Rinse the chicken under cold running water and pat dry with paper towels.

Place the chicken breasts in a large bowl and season with salt, pepper, and the thyme. Add the buttermilk and turn to coat; the chicken should be fully submerged. Cover and refrigerate for at least 8 hours or up to overnight.

Remove the chicken from the buttermilk and pat dry with paper towels; discard the buttermilk. Brush the skin side of the chicken with melted butter and generously season with salt and pepper.

Prepare a **CHARCOAL** or **GAS** grill for **DIRECT** grilling over **MEDIUM-HIGH** heat (pages 15–16). Brush and oil the grill grate. Have ready at hand a disposable aluminum roasting pan.

Place the chicken breasts directly over medium-high heat, skin side down, and grill until the skin is well marked and begins to crisp, 3–4 minutes. Turn the chicken over and grill until nicely charred, 3–4 minutes longer. Transfer the chicken, skin side up, to the aluminum pan. Place the pan on the edge of the grill where the heat is less intense, cover, and cook until cooked through, 15–20 minutes longer.

Transfer the breasts to a carving board and tent with aluminum foil. Let rest for a few minutes. Using a sharp boning knife, cut the meat away from the bones and cut on the diagonal into slices ¾ inch (2 cm) thick. Serve at once.

Bone-in chicken breast halves
4, or 1 chicken, about 3½ lb (1.75 kg), cut into 8 pieces

Coarse salt and ground pepper

Fresh thyme 1 tablespoon roughly chopped

Buttermilk 4 cups (32 fl oz/1 l)

Unsalted butter for brushing melted

TANDOORI CHICKEN WITH MINT RAITA

Mint Raita (page 267)

Cayenne pepper and paprika
1½ teaspoon *each*

Coarse salt and ground pepper

Skinless, boneless chicken breasts 6

Juice of 1 lemon

Small onion 1, roughly chopped

Garlic 2 cloves

Fresh ginger 2 tablespoons peeled and chopped

Whole-milk Greek-style yogurt
½ cup (4 oz/125 g)

Garam masala 1 teaspoon

Heavy (double) cream ¼ cup
(2 fl oz/60 ml)

Unsalted butter for brushing
melted

The flavor obtained by using an Indian clay tandoori oven can be approximated in a two-step process using a charcoal or gas grill. The secret is the double marinade: the chicken breasts are bathed first in lemon juice and then in a highly spiced yogurt marinade.

In a small bowl, make a spice rub by stirring together ½ teaspoon each of the cayenne, paprika, salt, and pepper.

Rinse the chicken under cold running water and pat dry with paper towels. Trim off the tenderloins from the chicken breasts; reserve for another use. Working with one piece at a time, lay a breast between two pieces of plastic wrap. With the bottom of a heavy pan, lightly pound the thickest part of the breast until flattened. Place the chicken in a large nonaluminum bowl and season with the spice rub, massaging it into the meat. Add the lemon juice and turn to coat well. Cover and refrigerate for 20–30 minutes.

To make the marinade: In a food processor, combine the onion, garlic, and ginger. Pulse several times to finely chop. Add the yogurt and the remaining spices and continue to pulse until well combined. Add the heavy cream, 1 tablespoon at a time, to thin the marinade.

Remove the chicken from the lemon juice and pat dry with paper towels; discard the lemon juice. Return the chicken to the bowl, add the marinade, and turn to coat. Cover and refrigerate, turning occasionally, for 1–2 hours. Remove from the refrigerator 15 minutes before grilling.

Prepare a **CHARCOAL** or **GAS** grill for **DIRECT** grilling over **MEDIUM-HIGH** heat (pages 15–16). Brush and oil the grill grate. Remove the chicken from the marinade, letting the excess drip back into the dish; discard the marinade.

Arrange the chicken breasts in the same direction on the grill grate. Grill the chicken directly over medium-high heat, turning once, until well marked and charred, 2–3 minutes per side. Move the chicken to the edge of the grill where the heat is less intense and brush with melted butter. Cover and grill until the chicken is firm to the touch and cooked through, 3–5 minutes longer. Serve with the raita.

ROTISSERIE CHICKEN

Fresh rosemary 10–12 sprigs

Fresh thyme 10–12 sprigs

Coarse salt and cracked pepper

Fryer chicken 1, 3–3½ lb (1.5–1.75 kg), neck and giblets removed

Wood chips 2 lb (1 kg), soaked for 30 minutes

Rosemary and thyme lend this spit-roasted chicken a distinctive Mediterranean flavor, but you can vary the herbs, depending on what you have available or growing in the garden.

Strip the leaves from half of the rosemary and thyme sprigs and roughly chop. Stir the chopped herbs together with 1 teaspoon salt, and ½ teaspoon pepper.

Generously season the chicken, inside and out, with salt and pepper. Carefully loosen the skin from the breast and legs with your fingers and massage the herb mixture under the skin. Stuff the remaining herb sprigs into the cavity of the bird.

Prepare a **CHARCOAL** or **GAS** grill for **ROTISSERIE GRILLING** over **MEDIUM-HIGH** heat (pages 15–16).

CHARCOAL: Rake the coals to the sides of the grill and place a drip pan in the fire bed. Add ½ inch (12 mm) water to the pan. Sprinkle half the wood chips over the coals. Thread the chicken onto the spit and secure it over the grill. Turn on the motor, cover, and spit-roast until the skin is browned and the juices run clear when the thigh is pierced, 45–75 minutes. Replenish the coals and chips every 20 minutes to maintain constant temperature and smoke.

GAS: Raise a burner to high. Heat a smoker box half full of wood chips until smoking; reduce heat to medium-low. Thread the chicken onto the rotisserie spit and secure it over the grill. Turn on the motor, cover, and spit-roast until the skin is browned and the juices run clear when the thigh is pierced with a knife, 45–75 minutes. Replenish the wood chips every 20 minutes to maintain constant smoke.

To test for doneness, insert an instant-read thermometer into the thickest part of the thigh away from the bone; it should register 170°F (77°C). The temperature will rise several more degrees while the chicken is resting. Transfer the chicken to a carving board and let rest for 10 minutes. Bring the whole chicken to the table on the carving board and carve in front of your guests.

TURKEY BURGERS

Turkey burgers satisfy a primal craving for meat without weighing you down. Use regular ground turkey, which is a mix of white and dark meat, as ground turkey breast is too lean for grilling.

Put the turkey in a large bowl and generously season with salt and pepper. Add the chicken stock, 1 tablespoon at a time, as needed to moisten the meat. Using wet hands, gently work the seasoning and stock into the meat, working quickly to keep the meat cool and being careful not to overwork it.

Divide the turkey mixture into six equal portions and form into patties 3½–4 inches (9–10 cm) in diameter and ¾ inch (2 cm) thick.

Place the patties on a plate, cover and refrigerate for 30 minutes.

Prepare a **CHARCOAL** or **GAS** grill for **DIRECT** grilling over **MEDIUM-HIGH** heat (pages 15–16). Brush and oil the grill grate.

Grill the burgers until well marked, 2–3 minutes. Turn the burgers, brush with the herb butter, and grill until nicely charred and cooked through, 4–6 minutes longer. Brush the insides of the rolls with melted butter and grill, cut sides down, until lightly toasted, 1 minute. Turn the rolls and grill for 30 seconds longer.

Serve the turkey burgers on the grilled rolls topped with lettuce, dill pickles, chutneys, and barbecue sauce, if using.

Spice-Herb Butter (page 252)

Ground (minced) turkey
1½ lb (500 g)

Salt and ground pepper

Chicken stock
¼ cup (2 fl oz/60 ml)

Sandwich rolls such as seeded Kaiser, ciabatta, or brioche
6, split, or white bread slices, cut into rounds using a large biscuit cutter

Iceberg or romaine (cos) lettuce ½ head, shredded

Dill pickles (pickled cucumbers) for serving, sliced

Basic Barbecue Sauce (page 231), Rhubarb Chutney (page 264), and Cranberry Chutney (page 264) for serving (optional)

GRILLED TURKEY

Apple-Bourbon Brine
(page 249)

Spice-Herb Butter (page 252)

Country-Style Gravy
(page 267)

Fresh whole turkey
1, 12–14 lb (6–7 kg), or 1 fresh
wild turkey, neck, giblets and
wing tips removed and turkey
dressed

Salt and ground white pepper

Carrots 3 large, peeled and
halved lengthwise

Celery 4 ribs

Yellow onions 2, peeled and
quartered

Wood chips or chunks 1–2 lb,
soaked for 30 minutes

The first Thanksgiving turkey was most likely cooked over a wood fire. Today's grilling enthusiasts have the benefit of modern equipment and techniques with which to improve upon our national holiday bird.

Brine the turkey (page 58). Season the turkey, inside and out, with salt and white pepper. Starting at the neck end, carefully loosen the skin from the breast with your fingers. Then, working from the cavity end, loosen the skin from the breast and legs. Massage the spice-herb butter under the skin; massage any remaining butter into the outside of the skin. Truss the turkey.

Prepare a **CHARCOAL** or **GAS** grill for **INDIRECT** grilling over **MEDIUM-LOW** heat (pages 15–16). Arrange the vegetables and the reserved herb sprigs in a large aluminum roasting pan. Place the turkey on top of the vegetables.

CHARCOAL: Sprinkle half of the wood chips over the coals. Place the pan with the turkey and vegetables on the cooler side of the grill, cover, and cook until the skin is nicely browned and the juices run clear when the thigh is pierced, 2½–3½ hours or 12–15 minutes per pound. Replenish the coals and wood chips and baste the turkey with its own juices every 30 minutes.

GAS: Raise a burner to high. Heat a smoker box half full of wood chips until smoking; reduce heat to medium-low. Place the pan with the turkey and vegetables over unlit burners, cover, and cook until the skin is browned and juices run clear when the thigh is pierced, 2½–3½ hours or 12–15 minutes per pound. Replenish wood chips and baste turkey with its own juices every 30 minutes.

To test for doneness, insert an instant-read thermometer into the thickest part of the thigh away from the bone; it should register 170°F (77°C). The breast meat should register at least 155°F (68°C).

Transfer the turkey to a carving board, tent with aluminum foil, and let rest for 20–30 minutes. Carve and serve with the country-style gravy alongside.

SMOKED TURKEY TENDERLOINS

Turkey tenderloin is a very lean poultry cut that benefits from grill-smoking over indirect heat.

To make the dry rub, pour the spices into a spice grinder and process into a coarse powder. Stir in the salt and set aside.

Rinse the turkey tenderloins under cold running water, pat dry, and lay between two sheets of plastic wrap on a work surface. Pound with the bottom of a heavy pan to a ¾-inch (2-cm) thickness. Season with half the dry rub. Arrange the tenderloins in a single layer in a nonaluminum dish. Pour the apple brine over the top, cover, and refrigerate for 1 hour. Remove the turkey from the brine and pat dry; discard the brine. Season the tenderloins with the remaining dry rub.

Prepare a **CHARCOAL** or **GAS** grill for **INDIRECT** grilling over **MEDIUM** heat (pages 15–16). Brush and oil the grill grate.

CHARCOAL: Rake the coals to the sides of the grill and place a drip pan with ½ inch (12 mm) water in the fire bed. Sprinkle half the wood chips over the coals. Place the tenderloins on the grate over the drip pan, cover, and cook, turning occasionally, for 15–20 minutes. Replenish coals and chips every 30 minutes. Remove the pan and rake the coals to the center of the grill. Place the tenderloins over the hottest part of the fire, brush with melted butter, and grill, turning once, 5–6 minutes longer.

GAS: Raise a burner to high. Fill a smoker box three-fourths full with wood chips and place on the burner until smoking; reduce heat to medium-low. Place a drip pan with ½ inch (12 mm) water directly over the heating elements. Place the tenderloins on the grate over the pan, cover, and cook, turning occasionally, for 15–20 minutes. Replenish the chips every 30 minutes. Place the tenderloins directly over the heating elements, brush with melted butter, and grill, turning once, 5–6 minutes longer.

Transfer the turkey tenderloins to a platter and serve with the cranberry chutney.

Cranberry Chutney (page 264)

Apple-Bourbon Brine (page 249) 1 cup (8 fl oz/ 250 ml)

DRY RUB

White peppercorns 1 tablespoon, toasted

Fennel seeds 1 tablespoon, toasted

Coriander seeds 1 tablespoon, toasted

Salt 2 tablespoons

Turkey tenderloins 4–5, 2½–3 lb (1.25–1.5 kg) total weight, trimmed

Unsalted butter for brushing melted

Wood chips or chunks 1 lb (500 g), soaked for 30 minutes

SMOKED TURKEY BREAST SALAD

Brown Sugar–Herb Rub (page 244)

Dijon Vinaigrette (page 200)

Boneless turkey breast half 1, skin-on, 3–4 lb (1.5–2 kg)

Apple juice 3 cups (24 fl oz/ 750 ml)

Butter (Boston) lettuce 1 head, torn into pieces

Small-leafed red lettuce 1 head

Arugula (rocket) 2 cups (2 oz/ 60 g)

Frisée 1 head, white part only

Belgian endives 2, cored and julienned

Radishes ½ cup (4 oz/125 g), very thinly sliced

Gruyère cheese 1½ lb (750 g), rind removed, cut into strips

Large eggs 6–8, hard-boiled, peeled, and quartered lengthwise

Flat-leaf (Italian) parsley, chives, marjoram, and tarragon ¼ cup (⅓ oz/10 g), chopped

Wood chips or chunks 1–2 lb (500 g–1 kg), soaked for 30 minutes

Slathered with Beer Mustard (page 263) or Caramelized Onion Jam (page 265), smoked turkey also makes a fantastic sandwich.

Remove the tenderloin from the breast and discard. Pat the turkey dry. Place the breast, skin side down, between two sheets of plastic wrap. With a heavy pan, pound until slightly flattened. Season all over and under the skin with half the rub. Roll the turkey into a uniform log, skin side out, and tie with 5 lengths of butcher's twine. Place in a deep nonaluminum pan. Pour the apple juice over the top and add enough water to partially submerge the turkey. Cover and refrigerate, turning occasionally, for 1 hour or up to overnight. Remove from the liquid 10 minutes before grilling and pat dry; discard the liquid. Season with the remaining rub.

Prepare a **CHARCOAL** or **GAS** grill for **INDIRECT** grilling over **MEDIUM** heat (pages 15–16). Brush and oil the grill grate.

CHARCOAL: Rake the coals to the sides and place a drip pan with ½ inch (12 mm) water in the fire bed. Sprinkle half the wood chips over the coals. Place the turkey on the grate, cover, and grill until cooked through, 1¼–1½ hours. Replenish coals and chips every 30 minutes.

GAS: Raise a burner to high. Heat a smoker box half full of wood chips until smoking; reduce heat to medium-low. Place a drip pan with ½ inch (12 mm) water directly over the heating elements. Place the turkey on the grate over the pan, cover, and grill until cooked through, 1¼–1½ hours. Replenish the chips every 30 minutes.

To test for doneness, insert an instant-read thermometer into the center of the breast; it should register 170–175°F (77–80°C). Transfer the turkey to a carving board, tent with aluminum foil, and let rest for 20–30 minutes before slicing.

In a bowl, combine the greens, half of the Dijon vinaigrette, and toss to coat. Divide among serving plates and top with the remaining ingredients. Drizzle with additional vinaigrette and serve.

DUCK BREAST WITH POMEGRANATE GLAZE

Blood oranges 4 or 2 large navel oranges

Pomegranate concentrate ½ cup (4 fl oz/125 ml)

Light agave syrup or honey 6 tablespoons (3 fl oz/90 ml)

Balsamic vinegar 1 tablespoon

Coarse salt and cracked pepper

Boneless, skin-on Muscovy or Pekin duck breasts 4, each 6–8 oz (185–250 g)

Pomegranate seeds ½ cup (3 oz/90 g) (optional)

Pomegranate concentrate is available in the beverage section of Middle Eastern, Asian, and Latin markets, as well as some gourmet supermarkets. Duck skin is rather fatty, but here the breasts are panfried prior to grilling to render some of the fat.

Using a knife, peel the oranges and, holding each orange over a colander set in a bowl, segment them. Leave the segments in the colander to drain; reserve the juice. In a small saucepan over medium heat, combine 4 tablespoons of the reserved orange juice, the pomegranate concentrate, agave syrup, vinegar, and a pinch of salt. Simmer until thick enough to coat the back of a spoon, 10–15 minutes.

Pat duck breasts dry with paper towels. Using a boning knife, trim the breasts to a uniform size, cutting away any excess fatty skin. Score the skin in a crosshatch pattern, without cutting into the flesh, at ½-inch (12-mm) intervals. Remove the tenderloins; discard or reserve for another use. Trim away any sinew from the undersides of the breasts. Generously season the breasts with salt and pepper.

Prepare a **CHARCOAL** or **GAS** grill for **DIRECT** grilling over **MEDIUM-HIGH** heat (pages 15–16). Preheat a cast-iron grill pan on the stove top over medium-high heat until smoking, 5–10 minutes. Working in batches, place the duck breasts, skin side down, in the preheated pan and cook until the fat begins to render, 4–5 minutes. Transfer the breasts to a shallow dish; reserve the rendered fat for another use. Pour half the pomegranate glaze over the duck and turn to coat. Keep the remaining glaze warm.

Place the duck on the grill, skin side down, directly over medium-high heat. Grill, turning once, until browned and cooked to your liking, 4–5 minutes per side for medium. During the last 2 minutes of cooking, brush with the remaining marinade.

Transfer the duck to a platter, tent with foil, and let rest for 5 minutes. Meanwhile, stir the orange segments and pomegranate seeds, if using, into the reserved glaze in the saucepan. Slice the duck breasts across the grain on the bias. Fan out the slices on individual plates and spoon the glaze on top.

DUCK WITH RED WINE SAUCE

Duck legs that are slowly cooked in their own fat until tender are one of southwestern France's great contributions to the culinary world. Paired with potatoes, this is bistro fare at its easiest.

Bring a pot three-fourths full of salted water to a boil. Add the potatoes and parboil just until cooked through, 10–12 minutes. Drain well. When cool enough to handle, cut the potatoes into wedges. Meanwhile, in a small saucepan over medium heat, melt the duck fat until liquefied, 1–2 minutes. In a large bowl, combine the potato wedges and 1–2 tablespoons of the duck fat and toss well to coat. Generously season with salt and pepper and toss with the parsley. Set aside.

To make the red wine sauce, strip the leaves from the herb sprigs; mince the leaves and reserve the sprigs. In a saucepan over high heat, bring the wine to a boil. Reduce the heat to a simmer and whisk in the demi-glace, 1 tablespoon at a time. Add the minced herbs, herb sprigs, vinegar, shallots, and garlic and simmer, stirring occasionally, until reduced by one-third, 8–10 minutes. Strain through a fine-mesh sieve into a small saucepan; discard the herbs. Taste and adjust the seasoning with salt and pepper. Keep warm.

Prepare a **CHARCOAL** or **GAS** grill for **DIRECT** grilling over **MEDIUM-HIGH** heat (pages 15–16). Brush and grease the grill grate with duck fat.

Place the duck legs on the grill, skin side down, directly over medium-high heat. Grill, turning once, until grill marks appear, 3–5 minutes per side. Move the duck legs to the edge of the grill where the heat is less intense to keep them warm. Grill the potato wedges over the hottest part of the fire, turning occasionally, until lightly charred and tender-crisp.

Mound the potatoes on a platter or divide among 6 individual plates. Top with grilled duck legs and spoon the red wine sauce over the top. Serve at once.

Coarse salt and cracked pepper

Thin-skinned potatoes
1½–2 lb (750–1 kg)

Duck fat or vegetable oil
¼ cup (2 oz/60 g)

Fresh flat-leaf (Italian) parsley 2–3 tablespoons minced

RED WINE SAUCE

Fresh herbs such as rosemary, thyme, or oregano 10 sprigs

Full-bodied red wine such as Cabernet Sauvignon 2–2½ cups (16–20 fl oz/500–625 ml)

Veal or poultry demi-glace
¼ cup (2 fl oz/60 ml)

Balsamic vinegar
1–2 tablespoons

Shallots 2, minced

Garlic 2 cloves, minced

Salt and pepper

Duck legs confit 6, trimmed

QUAIL WITH CIDER GLAZE

The best and simplest way to cook quail is on the grill, marinated in a simple apple cider and balsamic glaze and grill-roasted quickly to perfection. Count on one quail per person as an appetizer.

To make the cider glaze, in a bowl, stir together the apple juice concentrate, agave syrup, and vinegar. Pour half the glaze into a shallow nonaluminum dish large enough to accommodate the quail in a single layer. Pour the remaining half of the glaze into a small bowl and set aside.

Rinse the quail, inside and out, under cold water and pat dry with paper towels. To butterfly the quail, working with one at a time, place the bird, breast side down, on a work surface. Using kitchen shears, cut off the wing tips. Cut away the backbone on both sides, starting at the tail end and working towards the neck; discard the bones or reserve for stock. Open the bird like a book, pushing down on the breast bone until it cracks. Turn the bird over, skin side down, and use a small knife to remove the cartilage between the breasts. Cut the bird in half lengthwise along the center. You should have two halves, each with a leg, breast, and wing.

Season the quail halves with salt and pepper. Place in the dish with the glaze and turn to coat. Cover and refrigerate for at least 1 hour or up to 4 hours.

Prepare a **CHARCOAL** or **GAS** grill for **DIRECT** grilling over **MEDIUM-HIGH** heat (pages 15–16). Brush and grease the grill grate with duck fat.

Grill the quail directly over medium-high heat until nicely charred, 1–2 minutes. Turn and move to the edge of the grill where the heat is less intense. Brush with the remaining marinade, cover, and grill until browned and cooked through, 2–3 minutes longer. Serve with the reserved cider glaze spooned over the top.

CIDER GLAZE

Apple juice concentrate ¼ cup (2 fl oz/60 ml), thawed

Light agave syrup or honey ¼ cup (2 fl oz/60 ml)

Balsamic vinegar 2 tablespoons

Semi-boned quail 4, about 1 lb (500 g) total weight

Coarse salt and ground pepper

Duck fat or vegetable oil for brushing

CORNISH HENS WITH RHUBARB CHUTNEY

Rhubarb Chutney (page 264)

Coarse salt and ground pepper
¾ teaspoon *each*

Fresh rosemary 2 tablespoons
chopped or 1 tablespoon
dried rosemary

Fresh thyme 1–2 tablespoons
chopped or 1 tablespoon
dried thyme

Cornish game hens 2

Olive oil ¼ cup (2 fl oz/60 ml)

Duck fat or vegetable oil
for brushing

Wood chips or chunks
1 or 2 handfuls, soaked for
30 minutes

For delicious cornish hens, close your barbecue grill and use it like an oven for roasting—the added benefit of a hot, smoky fire gives the hens a good sear and charred, crispy skin.

In a small bowl, stir together the salt, pepper, rosemary, and thyme. If using dried herbs, use your fingers to crumble the herbs.

Pat the hens dry. Using kitchen shears, cut off the wing tips. Cut away each hen's backbone on both sides, starting at the tail end. Open the bird like a book, pushing down on the breast bone until it cracks. Turn the bird over and use a small knife to remove the cartilage between the breasts. Cut the bird in half lengthwise.

Arrange the hens in a single layer in a shallow roasting pan. Season both sides of the hens with the herb mixture. Pour the oil over the hens and turn to coat.

Prepare a **CHARCOAL** or **GAS** grill for **DIRECT** grilling over **MEDIUM-HIGH** heat (pages 15–16). Brush and grease the grill grate with the duck fat.

CHARCOAL: Sprinkle the wood chips over the coals. Grill the hens, skin side down, over the hottest part of the fire until juices begin to rise to surface of the meat, 7–9 minutes. Turn and grill until firm to the touch, 4–5 minutes. Move the hens to a cooler area, cover, and grill until deep golden brown, 10 minutes longer.

GAS: Raise a burner to high. Heat a smoker box half full of wood chips until smoking; reduce heat to medium-low. Grill the hens, skin side down, directly over the heating elements until juices begin to rise to surface of the meat, 7–9 minutes. Turn and grill until firm to the touch, 4–5 minutes. Move the hens to a cooler area, cover, and grill until golden brown, 10 minutes longer.

Insert an instant-read thermometer into the thickest part of the thigh meat; it should register 160°F (71°C). Transfer the hens to a platter and tent with foil. Let rest for 10 minutes, then serve with the rhubarb chutney.

Fish • Shellfish

SALMON WITH MISO GLAZE

MISO GLAZE

Light miso ⅓ cup
(3 fl oz/80 ml)

Mirin or sake ¼ cup
(2 fl oz/60 ml)

Light agave syrup or honey
3 tablespoons

Light brown sugar
1 tablespoon, firmly packed

Soy sauce 1 tablespoon

Salt and ground pepper

Green (spring) onions 12–14,
trimmed, including 2 inches
(5 cm) of tender green tops

Vegetable oil for brushing

Wild, skin-on salmon fillets
4, each about 3–4 oz
(90–125 g) and ¾–1 inch
(2–2.5 cm) thick, pin bones
removed

Salmon is best slightly underdone, still rosy pink in the center. If there is a danger of overcooking, move the fillets to an area of lower heat, brush with the remaining miso glaze, and finish cooking. For extra flavor, serve with a dollop of Wasabi Butter (page 253).

To make the miso glaze, in a small saucepan over medium-low heat, whisk together the miso, mirin, agave syrup, brown sugar, and soy sauce until the sugar is dissolved. Cook until slightly reduced and thick enough to coat the back of a spoon, 3–4 minutes. Season with salt and pepper. Let cool.

Prepare a **CHARCOAL** or **GAS** grill for **DIRECT** grilling over **MEDIUM-HIGH** heat (pages 15–16). Brush and oil the grill grate.

Brush the green onions with oil. Brush the salmon fillets with the miso glaze. Grill the salmon directly over medium-high heat, turning often and ending skin side down, until well marked and caramelized, 4–6 minutes total. During the last few minutes of cooking, grill the green onions directly over medium-high heat, turning often, until well marked and slightly wilted.

Transfer the salmon to warmed plates and arrange the grilled green onions on top. Serve at once.

HOME-CURED SMOKED SALMON

MAKES 10–12 SERVINGS

If you are an active angler, bring home your own fish and regale your friends with a fishing story or two while you enjoy one of the most appetizing dishes ever to come off a grill.

To make a curing mixture, in a large bowl, stir together the sugar, salt, pepper, bay leaves, and thyme. Pour one-third of the mixture in the bottom of a pan large enough to accommodate the salmon. Add the salmon, skin side down, and cover with the remaining mixture. Cover and refrigerate for at least 8 hours or preferably 12 hours or overnight. Remove from the refrigerator 30 minutes before grilling.

Prepare a **CHARCOAL** or **GAS** grill for **INDIRECT** grilling over **MEDIUM-HIGH** heat (pages 15–16). Wipe the curing mixture off the salmon and discard. Rinse the salmon under cold running water for 10–15 minutes and pat dry with paper towels.

CHARCOAL: Sprinkle half the wood chips over the coals. Place the salmon on a metal smoking rack and set the rack on the cooler side of the grill. Cover and grill until cooked through, 1–1¼ hours. Replenish the coals and wood chips every 30 minutes to maintain constant temperature and smoke.

GAS: Raise a burner to high. Heat a smoker box half full of wood chips until smoking; reduce heat to medium-low. Place the salmon on a metal smoking rack and set the rack on the cooler side of the grill. Cover and grill until cooked through, 1–1¼ hours. Replenish the wood chips every 30 minutes to maintain constant temperature and smoke.

Transfer the salmon to a cutting board. Serve at once, or tightly cover and refrigerate for up to 5 days. To serve, slice the salmon on the diagonal, starting at the tail section. Arrange on a large cutting board or chilled plate and serve with the flatbread crackers and the horseradish crème fraîche on the side.

Granulated sugar 2 cups (1 lb/500 g)

Salt 2 cups (1 lb/500 g)

Ground pepper ¼ cup (3 oz/90 g)

Bay leaves 4

Fresh thyme 1 tablespoon, roughly chopped

Wild salmon fillet 1, 2½–3 lb (1 kg–1.5 kg), pin bones removed

Flatbread crackers for serving (optional)

Horseradish Crème Fraîche (page 257) for serving

Hardwood chips 2–3 handfuls, soaked for 30 minutes

172   FISH • SHELLFISH

TUNA WITH OLIVE & ARTICHOKE RELISH

The Mediterranean Sea meets the Pacific Ocean in this California wine country classic using the freshest sushi-grade tuna, cured olives, ripe tomatoes, and California baby artichokes. Be sure to oil your grill grate well to avoid having the fish stick to it. Tapenade Relish (page 263), also makes a nice accompaniment to this dish.

Crush the anchovies into a paste.

To make the artichoke relish, in a heavy-bottomed 4-quart (128 fl oz/4 l) sauce pan over medium heat, combine 3 tablespoons of the olive oil, the anchovies, and onion and sauté over medium heat until the mixture is fragrant and onions are soft, 4–5 minutes. Remove from the heat, stir in the red bell pepper, olives, artichoke wedges, tomato, tomato paste, and the remaining 1 tablespoon olive oil. Season with salt, pepper, and smoked paprika. Toss to coat, fold in the parsley, and transfer to a bowl. Let stand at room temperature while grilling the fish.

Prepare a **CHARCOAL** or **GAS** grill for **DIRECT** grilling over **MEDIUM-HIGH** heat (pages 15–16). Brush and oil the grill grate.

When the grill is heated, throw the herb sprigs on the hot coals (or heating elements of a gas grill) to create fragrant smoke.

Grill the tuna steaks over the hottest part of the grill, turning once, until seared on the outside with attractive grill marks and rare in the center, 2–3 minutes per side. Do not overcook. Transfer the tuna steaks to individual serving plates and spoon some of the olive artichoke relish over the top, passing the rest at the table.

Oil-packed anchovies 2, drained and blotted dry

Olive oil ¼ cup (2 fl oz/60 ml)

White onion 1 small, diced

Red bell pepper (capsicum) 1, grilled, peeled, cored, seeded, and diced

Mixed olives 1 cup (5 oz/ 155 g), pitted and chopped

Baby artichokes 12, trimmed, parboiled, drained, grilled, and cut into wedges

Tomato 1, peeled, seeded and diced

Tomato paste 1 tablespoon

Salt and ground pepper

Smoked paprika ½ teaspoon

Fresh flat leaf (Italian) parsley 2 tablespoons, roughly chopped

Fresh rosemary and lemon thyme sprigs

Sushi-grade tuna steaks 4, each 1 inch (2.5 cm) thick, 2½–3 lb (1.25–1.5 kg) total weight

HALIBUT WRAPPED IN FIG LEAVES

Skinless, boneless halibut fillets or other firm-fleshed white fish 4, each 3–4 oz (90–125 g) and ¾–1 inch (2–2.5 cm) thick, thawed if frozen

Coarse salt and ground pepper

Fig leaves 4 large

Olive oil ¼ cup (2 fl oz/60 ml)

Fig trees produce fragrant leaves that can be used as a jacket for fish on the grill, imparting a tropical coconut flavor. If you don't live in an area where fig trees are plentiful, look for them at a garden center or use banana or grape leaves instead. The leaves spoil quickly, so use them the day they are plucked from the tree.

Season the fish with salt and pepper. Arrange the fig leaves on a work surface and brush the inside of each with oil. Place a fish fillet in the center of each leaf and brush the fish with oil. Working with one fillet at a time, wrap each fish in the fig leaf, starting at the wide, bottom end and rolling and folding the sides over to enclose the fish. Secure the packets with toothpicks, if necessary. Place the packets on a plate and refrigerate until ready for use.

Prepare a **CHARCOAL** or **GAS** grill for **INDIRECT** grilling over **MEDIUM** heat (pages 15–16). Brush and oil the grill grate and a fish-grilling basket, if desired.

Arrange the fish packets on the rack or in the basket on the side of the grill where the heat is less intense. Cover and grill, turning once, until the leaves are lightly charred and the fish is cooked through, 5–6 minutes per side. During the last few minutes of cooking, move the packets over direct heat and grill until well marked.

Transfer the grilled fish packets to individual plates or a platter and serve at once. (The fig leaves are not edible.)

SNAPPER FISH TACOS

Jalapeño chiles 2, quartered
lengthwise and seeded

Vegetable oil for brushing
1 tablespoon, plus more for
brushing

Skinless, boneless snapper or
other firm white fish fillets
6, each 4–5 oz (125–155 g),
thawed if frozen

Salt and ground pepper

Corn tortillas 12–16, each
6 inches (15 cm) in diameter

Limes 2, cut into wedges

Iceberg lettuce ½ head,
shredded

Fresh salsa 1½ cups
(9 oz/280 g)

Onions, tomatoes, cucumbers,
and fresh cilantro (fresh
coriander) for serving,
chopped (optional)

Hot-pepper sauce

Hardwood chips 1 handful,
soaked for 30 minutes

*Don't worry if the fillets break during grilling; they will be flaked into
smaller pieces before serving. If this occurs, transfer them to a sheet
of heavy-duty foil and finish grilling over a less hot part of the grill.*

Prepare a **CHARCOAL** or **GAS** grill for **DIRECT** grilling over **MEDIUM-HIGH** heat
(pages 15–16). Brush and oil the grill grate.

Toss the chiles in a small bowl with the oil. Brush the fish with oil and season
with salt and pepper. Working in batches, grill the tortillas until warmed through,
1–2 minutes. Wrap in foil or a kitchen towel to keep them warm.

CHARCOAL: Sprinkle the wood
chips over the coals. Place the
chiles over the hottest part of the
fire. Grill, turning once, until nicely
charred, 1–2 minutes per side. Grill
the fish over the hottest part of the
fire until opaque and nicely charred,
3–5 minutes. Using a wide spatula,
carefully turn the fish and grill until
cooked through, 3–4 minutes longer.

GAS: Raise a burner to high. Heat
a smoker box half full of wood
chips until smoking; reduce heat to
medium-low. Place the chiles over
the heating elements. Grill, turning
once, until nicely charred, 1–2
minutes per side. Grill the fish over
the heating elements until opaque
and nicely charred, 3–5 minutes.
Using a wide spatula, carefully
turn the fish and grill until cooked
through, 3–4 minutes longer.

Roughly chop the grilled chiles and place them in small bowl. Squeeze 1 or 2 lime
wedges over them and stir to coat.

Transfer the fish to a board and flake each fillet into small pieces. To assemble
the grilled fish tacos, place several pieces of fish and some grilled chiles atop
2 stacked warm corn tortillas. Top with the lettuce, salsa, and other toppings of
your choice. Garnish with a few dashes of hot-pepper sauce and serve at once.

GRILLED WHOLE FISH

Grilling a whole fish is the final frontier of mastering the modern grill. For the anglers among us, there is almost no greater culinary pleasure than a perfectly grilled fresh fish landed by the griller himself.

With a very sharp knife, score the skin on both sides of the fish on the diagonal at 1-inch (2.5 cm) intervals. Place in a shallow dish.

In a small bowl, stir together the chopped rosemary, chopped thyme, and garlic paste. Rub the herb-garlic paste all over the outside and inside of the fish. Season with salt and pepper. Pour the vermouth and olive oil over the fish in the pan, turn to coat, and let stand for 30 minutes.

Prepare a **CHARCOAL** or **GAS** grill for **DIRECT** grilling over **MEDIUM-HIGH** heat (pages 15–16). Brush and oil the grill grate and a fish-grilling basket, if desired.

Remove the fish from the marinade; discard the marinade. Stuff the fish cavities with a few of the lemon slices and the rosemary and thyme sprigs.

Arrange the fish on the rack or in the basket directly over medium-high heat. Grill, turning once, until nicely charred and cooked through, 3–4 minutes per side. During the last few minutes of grilling, grill the remaining lemon slices over the hottest part of the fire, turning once, until lightly browned, 1–2 minutes per side.

Transfer the grilled trout to individual plates or a serving platter, garnish with the grilled lemon slices, and serve at once.

Rainbow steelhead or rainbow trout 4, about 2 lb (1 kg) each, cleaned

Fresh rosemary 2 tablespoons roughly chopped, plus 12 sprigs

Fresh thyme 2 tablespoons roughly chopped, plus 12 sprigs

Garlic 3 cloves, crushed into a paste

Salt and ground pepper

Dry vermouth or white wine ½ cup (4 fl oz/125 ml)

Olive oil ½ cup (4 fl oz/ 125 ml)

Lemons 2, sliced into rounds

USING FRESH HERBS ON THE GRILL

If using fresh woody herbs, such as rosemary and thyme, save the sprigs after you pluck off the leaves and toss them onto the fire to add a subtle flavor to the smoke that surrounds and imbues the food.

CALAMARI WITH MEYER LEMON AIOLI

Meyer Lemon Aioli (page 256)

Small calamari, tentacles and bodies, thawed if frozen 2 lb (1 kg)

Lemons 2

Olive oil ½ cup (4 fl oz/ 125 ml)

Red wine vinegar 1 tablespoon

Garlic 3 cloves, minced

Red pepper flakes 1 teaspoon

Coarse salt 2 teaspoons

Ground pepper 1 teaspoon

Hot-pepper sauce

Fresh flat-leaf (Italian) parsley ¼ cup (⅓ oz/10 g) finely chopped

Red pear-shaped cherry tomatoes 10–12, halved lengthwise (optional)

Grilled calamari makes a delicious addition to a salad, a selection of antipasti, or a mixed seafood grill. For even cooking, weigh the calamari down with a well-cleaned preheated cast-iron pan or a brick wrapped in heavy-duty aluminum foil.

Place the calamari in a colander, rinse under cold running water, pat dry. Pull the tentacles off the bodies. Cut any large tentacles in half and any bodies longer than 4 inches (10 cm) into 1½–2 inch (4–5 cm) pieces. Cut away the small beaks from the tentacles; discard the beaks. Drain the calamari in the colander.

Using a microplane grater, grate the zest from one of the lemons; halve and juice the other lemon.

In a medium bowl, whisk together the lemon zest, ¼ cup (2 fl oz/60 ml) of the lemon juice, oil, vinegar, garlic, red pepper flakes, salt, pepper, and hot-pepper sauce to taste. Add the calamari and toss to coat.

Prepare a **CHARCOAL** or **GAS** grill for **DIRECT** grilling over **HIGH** heat (pages 15–16). Preheat a large cast-iron pan over the hottest part of the fire. Brush the bottom of the pan and the grill grate with oil.

Arrange the calamari on the grill directly over high heat. Place the preheated pan on top of the calamari to flatten them. Grill, turning once and brushing with any remaining oil mixture, until opaque and nicely charred, 1–2 minutes per side.

Transfer the grilled calamari to a cutting board and cut into bite-sized rings and pieces while still hot off the grill. Mound onto a platter and garnish with the parsley and tomatoes, if using. Drizzle the Meyer lemon aioli on top or serve it on the side as a dipping sauce. Serve at once.

SWEET & SOUR SHRIMP SKEWERS

Shrimp skewers are very easy to put together and can be seasoned and sauced in a variety of ways with just a few ingredients from your fridge and pantry. Here, large shrimp get a sesame oil, lime, and chile marinade to add big flavor and to keep them moist on the grill.

Soak the bamboo skewers in water for 30 minutes.

With the side of a chef's knife, crush the garlic into a paste with 1 teaspoon salt. To make a sweet and sour sauce, in a small saucepan over medium heat, combine the garlic paste, 3 tablespoons of the sesame oil, ketchup, soy sauce, vinegar, honey, ginger, and chile sauce and bring to a boil. Simmer, whisking constantly, until thick and syrupy, 3–5 minutes. Strain through a fine-mesh sieve into a bowl, pushing down on the solids with the back of spoon to extract all of their flavor; discard the solids. Let the sauce cool.

Place the shrimp in a colander, rinse under cold running water, and pat dry with paper towels. In a large bowl, combine the shrimp, lime zest and juice, remaining 2 tablespoons sesame oil, red pepper flakes, and ½ teaspoon each salt and pepper. Toss to coat. Cover and refrigerate for 30–60 minutes.

Prepare a **CHARCOAL** or **GAS** grill for **DIRECT** grilling over **MEDIUM-HIGH** heat (pages 15–16). Brush and oil the grill grate.

Starting at the thickest end, thread the shrimp onto the skewers; reserve the marinade. Working in batches, grill the shrimp skewers over the hottest part of the fire, turning once and brushing with the reserved marinade, until the shrimp are bright red and nicely charred, 1–2 minutes per side.

Transfer the skewers to small individual plates or a large platter. Spoon some of the sweet and sour sauce over the top, garnish with the green onions and toasted sesame seeds, and serve with the remaining sweet and sour sauce on the side.

Garlic 2 cloves

Coarse salt and ground pepper

Asian sesame oil 5 tablespoons (3 fl oz/80 ml)

Tomato ketchup 2 tablespoons

Soy sauce and rice wine vinegar 2 tablespoons *each*

Honey 2 tablespoons

Fresh ginger 1 tablespoon finely grated

Thai sweet chile sauce 1 tablespoon

Large shrimp (prawns) 24–30, 1½–2 lb (750 g–1 kg) total weight, peeled and deveined with tail tips, thawed if frozen

Zest and juice of 1 lime

Red pepper flakes 1 tablespoon

Green (spring) onions 2–3, trimmed

Sesame seeds 2–3 tablespoons, toasted

Bamboo skewers 12–18

MIXED SEAFOOD GRILL

Spice-Herb Butter (page 252) or Lemon Tarragon Butter (page 253)

Seasoning Mix (page 249)

Large shrimp (prawns) 2½ lb (1.25 kg), about 25, thawed if frozen

Sea scallops 2 lb (1 kg), about 20, side muscle removed, thawed if frozen

Large oysters 10

Sardines 8 fresh, cleaned

Lobster tails 4, parboiled for 3 minutes and split in half lengthwise

Bone-in halibut steaks 2, each 6–8 oz (185–250 g)

Lemon wedges

Worcestershire sauce

Hot-pepper sauce

Fresh flat-leaf (Italian) parsley ½ cup (¾ oz/20 g) chopped

This seafood extravaganza is perfect for a crowd of culinary enthusiasts who don't mind getting a little messy. Feel free to substitute whichever seafood varieties are freshest in your area. Wash it all down with plenty of cold beer or a crisp white wine.

Place the shrimp, scallops, and oysters in a colander, rinse under cold running water, and pat dry with paper towels. Rinse the sardines under cold running water and pat dry with paper towels. Trim off the fins, leaving the heads and tails on.

Prepare a **CHARCOAL** or **GAS** grill for **DIRECT** grilling over **MEDIUM-HIGH** (pages 15–16). Brush and oil the grill grate. Have ready 1 or 2 large serving platters.

Season the shrimp, scallops, lobster tails, and halibut with the seasoning mix and brush with the spice-herb or lemon tarragon butter. Season the sardines with the seasoning mix and brush with oil. If the shrimp and scallops are small enough to fall through the grill grate, thread them onto metal skewers.

Grill the lobster tails and halibut steaks directly over medium-high heat, turning once, until opaque and nicely charred, 3–4 minutes per side. Meanwhile, grill the oysters over indirect heat until they open slightly, about 2 minutes. Using tongs, transfer the oysters to a work surface covered with a kitchen towel. With a pointed shucking knife, carefully shuck the oysters of their top shell. Place the oysters over the hottest part of the fire until bubbling, 2–3 minutes. Grill the shrimp, scallops, and sardines over the hottest part of the fire, turning once, until charred and cooked through, 2–3 minutes per side for the shrimp and scallops and 3–5 minutes per side for the sardines. Season the seafood with the seasoning mix and brush with the remaining spice-herb or lemon tarragon butter as it cooks.

Transfer the seafood to the serving platters and serve with the lemon wedges, Worcestershire, hot-pepper sauce, and chopped parsely.

SALT & PEPPER SHRIMP

Shrimp on the grill have never been this good and this variation on a classic Vietnamese dish is easy to prepare and messy to eat! Look for good-quality shrimp at the fish counter of a reputable grocery store.

Place the shrimp in a colander, rinse under cold running water, and pat dry. In a large bowl, combine the shrimp, lime juice, salt, black, white, and cayenne peppers, and chile powder and toss to coat. Add a splash of vermouth and the ¼ cup (2 fl oz/60 ml) oil and toss to coat. Cover and refrigerate until ready to use.

Prepare a **CHARCOAL** or **GAS** grill for **DIRECT** grilling over **MEDIUM-HIGH** heat (pages 15–16). Brush and oil the grill grate.

Working in batches, grill the shrimp directly over medium-high heat, turning once, until bright red and nicely charred, 2–3 minutes per side. Transfer the shrimp to a platter and tent with aluminum foil.

Transfer the grilled shrimp to individual plates. Serve at once with the saffron aioli.

HOW TO CRACK WHOLE PEPPERCORNS

Lay a large sheet of parchment or wax paper on a cutting board that sits firmly on a work surface. Place 2–3 tablespoons peppercorns in the center and fold the edges over to make a small pouch. Using a heavy sauté pan or Dutch oven, apply pressure and rock back and forth to crack the peppercorns. Strain through a coarse-mesh sieve and repeat the process. Keep freshly cracked pepper handy for seasoning grilled steaks, seafood, chops, and for garnishing salads.

Large shrimp (prawns) 4 lb (2 kg), peeled and thawed if frozen

Fresh lime juice 2 tablespoons

Coarse salt 1 tablespoon

Cracked black pepper (see note) 1 tablespoon

Cracked white pepper (see note) 1 tablespoon

Cayenne pepper 1 teaspoon

Chile powder ½ teaspoon

Dry vermouth

Olive oil ¼ cup (2 fl oz/60 ml), plus extra for brushing

Saffron Aioli (page 257) for serving (optional)

WHOLE LOBSTER

Live Maine lobsters
2, 1½–2 lb (750 g–1 kg) each,
or 2 frozen spiny lobster
tails, thawed

GARLIC-LEMON BUTTER

Unsalted butter ½ cup
(4 oz/125 g)

Garlic cloves 3, minced

**Zest and juice of 1 lemon,
plus 2 lemons thinly sliced
into rounds**

Salt and ground pepper

**Fresh herbs such as chervil,
flat-leaf (Italian) parsley,
tarragon, or any combination**
1 tablespoon *each*, minced

Lobsters are great on the grill. When using live lobsters, be brave and take on the role of executioner, a daunting but necessary task. Don't be squeamish about dispatching live lobsters; a quick downward stroke with a knife kills them instantly. It's over in less than a second.

Bring a large pot three-fourths full of salted water to a boil. Have ready a bowl of ice water large enough to fit the lobsters.

On a cutting board, use the point of a chef's knife to cut an incision through each lobster head shell about 1 inch (2.5 cm) from the eyes, pushing down hard through the shell to instantly kill the lobster. Immediately plunge the lobsters into the pot and cook for 2 minutes. Transfer to the ice bath. When cool enough to handle, split the lobsters in half lengthwise. Remove the intestinal vein from the tails, the grain sacs from the heads, and any green tomalley from the bodies; reserve any black egg sacs in a small bowl.

Pour ¼ cup (2 fl oz/60 ml) boiling water over the egg sacs and, using a fork, gently break the membrane to release the roe; it will turn bright red in the hot water. Strain through a sieve and let dry on paper towel.

To make the garlic-lemon butter, in a small saucepan over medium heat, melt the butter. Stir in the garlic and the lemon zest and juice. Add salt and pepper to taste, herbs, and 2 tablespoons of the reserved lobster eggs, if any. Keep warm.

Prepare a **CHARCOAL** or **GAS** grill for **DIRECT** grilling over **MEDIUM-HIGH** heat (pages 15–16). Brush and oil the grill grate.

Brush the cut side of each lobster half with the garlic-lemon butter. Place the lobsters, cut side down, directly on the grill. Cover and grill until the flesh is opaque and firm to the touch, 5–6 minutes. Grill the lemon slices over the hottest part of the fire until lightly charred, 1–2 minutes per side.

Brush the lobsters with garlic-lemon butter and transfer to a serving platter. Garnish with grilled lemon slices and serve at once.

SCALLOPS WITH AVOCADO SALSA

Large scallops are increasingly easy to find at better fish stores and supermarkets, frozen or thawed. Look for natural "wild" scallops without additives or preservatives, which can impart an unpleasant chemical taste to the scallop's sweet, delicate flesh.

To make the avocado salsa, in a small bowl, whisk together 2 tablespoons of the olive oil, 3 tablespoons lime juice, 2 tablespoons of the tequila, the chipotles and adobo sauce, agave syrup, and 1 teaspoon each salt and pepper. In a medium bowl, combine the avocado, white and red onions, tomatoes, jalapeño, pumpkin seeds, cumin, and cilantro. Pour the lime-tequila mixture over the top and gently stir to coat, being careful not to break up the avocado.

Prepare a **CHARCOAL** or **GAS** grill for **DIRECT** grilling over **MEDIUM-HIGH** heat (pages 15–16). Brush and oil the grill grate.

Cut the tortillas into 3-inch (7.5-cm) rounds with a biscuit cutter and lightly brush each with oil. Remove the side muscle from each scallop.

In a large bowl, whisk together the remaining ¼ cup olive oil, remaining 2 tablespoons tequila, and lime zest and remaining juice. Lightly season the scallops on both sides with salt and pepper. Just before grilling, add the scallops to the bowl and toss briefly to coat. Transfer to a plate.

Grill the scallops directly over medium-high heat, 2 minutes per side, until grill marks appear and the scallops are completely cooked through. Grill the tortillas until the edges are crisp, turning once, 1–2 minutes per side.

Spread the avocado salsa on the tortilla rounds and top each with a scallop. Serve at once.

Extra-virgin olive oil ¼ cup (2 fl oz/60 ml) plus 2 tablespoons

Zest and juice of 2 limes

Tequila ¼ cup (2 fl oz/60 ml)

Canned chipotle chiles in adobo sauce 2, seeded and finely chopped, plus 1 teaspoon adobo sauce

Light agave syrup 1 teaspoon

Salt and ground pepper

Ripe avocados 2, pitted, peeled, and diced

White onion and red onion ½ cup (2½ oz/75 g) *each*, diced

Tomatoes 2, seeded, and diced

Jalapeño or serrano chile 1, seeded and finely diced

Pumpkin seeds 3 tablespoons

Ground cumin 1 teaspoon

Fresh cilantro (fresh coriander) ½ cup (¾ oz/20 g) finely chopped

Corn tortillas 12, each 6 inches (15 cm) in diameter

Sea scallops 2 lb (1 kg)

GRILLED OYSTERS WITH BARBECUE SAUCE

**Basic Barbecue Sauce
(page 231)**

Oysters 24, large

Worcestershire sauce

Hot-pepper sauce

Lemon wedges for garnish

Grilling oysters is a three-step process: The oysters are steamed briefly to open them, shucked of their top shells, and finished on the grill. Barbecue sauce is a tangy last-minute addition.

Prepare a **CHARCOAL** or **GAS** grill for **DIRECT** grilling over **HIGH** heat (pages 15–16). Brush the grill grate.

Arrange half of the oysters, bottom shell down, in a disposable aluminum roasting pan. Add ¼ cup (2 fl oz/60 ml) water and cover tightly with aluminum foil.

Place the roasting pan with the oysters on the grill directly over high heat and steam until the oysters open, about 2 minutes. Using tongs, transfer the oysters to a work surface covered with a kitchen towel. Repeat to steam the remaining oysters. With a pointed shucking knife, carefully shuck the oysters of their top shells. Cut under the oyster muscle and flip the oysters over. Top each oyster with 1 teaspoon barbecue sauce, 1 drop of Worcestershire, and 1 drop of hot-pepper sauce. Grill the oysters over the hottest part of the fire until the sauce bubbles, 30–60 seconds.

Using tongs, carefully transfer the grilled oysters to a platter. Garnish with lemon wedges and serve at once with barbecue sauce, Worcestershire, and hot-pepper sauce.

On the Side

BUTTERMILK COLESLAW

**Buttermilk Dressing
(page 260)**

Green and red cabbages
½ head *each*

Large carrot 1

Red onion ½

Shallots 2

Golden raisins (sultanas)
½ cup (3 oz/90 g)

White vinegar
3 tablespoons

Salt and ground white pepper

**Fresh flat-leaf (Italian)
parsley leaves and chives for
garnish** chopped

*A barbecue isn't a barbecue without coleslaw, and this version
offers rich and tangy flavor with a homemade buttermilk dressing,
enlivened with fresh herbs and raisins.*

Core and thinly shred the cabbages. Using a mandoline (if desired), peel and thinly
julienne the carrot. Very thinly slice the red onion and shallots.

Place the raisins in a small bowl. Add warm water to cover and soak until plump,
about 30 minutes; drain. In another small bowl, combine the carrot, onion,
shallots, and vinegar and toss to coat.

In a large salad bowl, toss together the green and red cabbage. Add the raisins,
carrot-vinegar mixture, and buttermilk dressing and toss to coat. Taste and adjust
the seasoning with salt and pepper. Garnish with the parsley and chives and
refrigerate until ready to serve.

THREE-CHEESE MACARONI & CHEESE

For this recipe, a pasta with ridges will hold the sauce best. Look for artisanal or whole-grain dried pasta, which has a better flavor than standard boxed versions. This dish is finished under the broiler (grill).

Bring a large pot three-fourths full of water to a boil. Salt generously and add the pasta, stirring with a large spoon to prevent clumping. Return to a boil and cook until al dente, 8–10 minutes; the pasta should be slightly underdone. Drain into a colander, then transfer back to the pot and toss with half the melted butter.

Preheat the broiler (grill) to medium-high. Brush the sides and bottom of a large gratin dish or a 9-by-13-inch (23-by-33-cm) baking pan with melted butter.

In a bowl, combine the oil and remaining melted butter. Stir in the bread crumbs, parsley, thyme, garlic paste, and ½–¾ cup (2–3 oz/60–90 g) of the pecorino. Taste and adjust the seasoning with salt and pepper. Coat the bottom and sides of the buttered gratin dish with some of the bread crumb mixture.

In a large, heavy saucepan over medium-high heat, bring the cream just to a boil, being careful not to let it boil over. Reduce the heat to medium-low and add ¾ cup (3 oz/90 g) pecorino and the American and Cheddar cheeses. Whisk gently until smooth, 1–2 minutes. Add the cooked pasta and stir to coat. Taste and adjust the seasoning with salt and pepper.

Transfer the pasta to the prepared gratin dish and add the remaining bread crumb mixture over the top. Broil, rotating the pan halfway through cooking, until the bread crumbs are toasted golden brown, 4–5 minutes. Serve at once.

HOW TO COOK PASTA AL DENTE

All dried pasta should be cooked until al dente, which means "to the tooth." To test for doneness, lift a small amount of pasta from the pot with a slotted spoon and place in a small bowl of cold water. Let the pasta cool and take a bite. It should be soft on the outside and firm on the inside. If it is not ready, continue cooking 1–2 minutes longer and test again.

Dried pasta such as macaroni or penne rigate 1 lb (500 g)

Unsalted butter 4 tablespoons (2 oz/60 g), melted

Olive oil ¼ cup (2 fl oz/60 ml)

Fresh bread crumbs 1½ cups (3 oz/90 g)

Fresh flat-leaf (Italian) parsley ¼ cup (⅓ oz/10 g) minced

Fresh thyme 1 tablespoon minced

Garlic 2 cloves, crushed into a paste with ½ teaspoon salt

Pecorino romano cheese 1 chunk, 6–8 oz (185–250 g), very finely grated

Coarse salt and ground pepper

Heavy (double) cream 2 cups (16 fl oz/500 ml)

Orange or white unprocessed American cheese 5 slices (5 oz/155 g)

Sharp Cheddar cheese 1¼ cups (5 oz/155 g), shredded

ORZO SALAD

This salad of rice-shaped pasta is perfect for summer entertaining. It is large enough to feed a hungry crowd and is even more delicious the next day when the flavors have blended together.

Bring a large pot three-fourths full of salted water to a boil. Have ready a bowl full of ice and cold water. Add the orzo, stirring with a large spoon to prevent sticking. Bring to a boil and cook the orzo until al dente, 8–10 minutes. During the last minute of cooking, add the peas. Drain into a colander. Pour the orzo and peas into the ice bath and drain again. Transfer to a salad bowl. Drizzle with the 1–2 tablespoons extra-virgin olive oil and stir to coat. Cover and refrigerate.

To make the vinaigrette, combine the remaining ¼ cup olive oil and the grapeseed oil in a glass measuring cup. In a nonaluminum bowl, whisk together the vinegar and mustard. Add the oils in a slow steady stream, whisking constantly. Taste and adjust the seasoning with salt and pepper. Set vinaigrette aside.

Prepare a **CHARCOAL** or **GAS** grill for **DIRECT** grilling over **HIGH** heat (pages 15–16). Brush and oil the grill grate and a vegetable-grilling basket.

Brush the onions and bell peppers with olive oil. Arrange the onions in the grilling basket.

Grill the bell peppers directly over high heat, turning occasionally, until nicely charred on all sides. Transfer the grilled peppers to a bowl, cover, and let steam for 10 minutes. Meanwhile, place the grilling basket with the onions directly over high heat. Grill, turning once, until nicely charred on both sides, about 8–10 minutes per side. Transfer the grilled onions to a plate.

When the peppers are cool enough to handle, using your fingers or a paring knife, peel them and discard the skins. Seed and dice the peppers. Add the peppers, onions, parsley, and vinaigrette to the bowl with the orzo and peas and toss to coat. Taste and adjust the seasoning with salt and pepper. Garnish with the tomatoes and serve.

Dried orzo pasta 1 lb (500 g)

Fresh English peas 1 cup (5 oz/155 g)

Extra-virgin olive oil 1–2 tablespoons plus ¼ cup (2 fl oz/60 ml)

DIJON VINAIGRETTE
Grapeseed oil ½ cup (4 fl oz/125 ml)

Red wine vinegar 2 tablespoons

Dijon mustard 1 tablespoon

Salt and ground pepper

Red and white onions, 1 *each,* sliced ½ inch (12 mm) thick

Red, orange, and yellow bell peppers (capsicums) 1 *each*

Fresh flat-leaf (Italian) parsley 1 cup (1⅓ oz/40 g) minced

Salt and ground pepper

Small heirloom tomatoes, 12, about 3 lb (1.5 kg) total weight, cored and quartered

BAKED BEANS WITH PANCETTA

Dried cannellini beans
2 cups (1 lb/500 g) or 2 cans
(15 oz/450 g) white kidney
beans

Extra-virgin olive oil
¼ cup (2 fl oz/60 ml),
plus 2 tablespoons

Pancetta ¼ lb (500 g), ⅛ inch
(3 mm) thick, diced

Small onion 1, peeled and
quartered

Carrot and celery stalk 1 *each*
peeled, cut into 3 chunks

Garlic 4 cloves, diced

Fresh sage 3 leaves

Vegetable stock or water
4–6 cups (32 fl oz/1 l)

Coarse salt and ground pepper

Tomato paste 2 tablespoons

**Fresh flat-leaf (Italian)
parsley** 1-2 tablespoons
chopped

Tomato 1, peeled, seeded, and
cut into ¼-inch (6-mm) dice

White beans and pork are a classic Tuscan combination, brightened with fresh herbs and flavorful olive oil. Pancetta is natural Italian bacon from the pork belly that is brined with garlic and herbs and rolled into a log. White kidney beans and Great Northern beans in cans are a convenient alternative to dried cannellini beans.

Pick over and discard any damaged beans. Rinse the dried beans in a sieve under cold running water, transfer to a large bowl and add enough cold water to cover by 1 inch (2.5 cm). Let soak for at least 8 hours or overnight.

When ready to cook, preheat oven to 350°F (180°C), with a rack set in the middle of the oven. Drain the beans well. If using canned beans, drain, rinse and pick over beans to remove any that are damaged or broken.

In an enamel-covered pot, over medium heat, warm 2 tablespoons olive oil. Add the diced pancetta and sauté until tender crisp and some fat has rendered. Tilt the pot and discard all but 2 tablespoons of the fat in the pot, leaving the pancetta. Add the onion, carrot, celery, garlic, sage and the beans. Add the vegetable stock (or water) to cover. Season the beans with 1 teaspoon pepper. Bring the pot to a simmer, cover and transfer to the oven. Bake until the beans are tender, 1–1½ hours. If using canned beans, reduce the cooking time by half.

Transfer the beans on top of the stove and put on medium heat and bring to a gentle simmer.

In a small bowl, whisk the tomato paste with 1 cup (8 fl oz/250 ml) of the hot bean cooking liquid. Add the tomato paste to the pot, stirring to incorporate. Season to taste with salt and pepper. Turn off the heat and let the beans cool to room temperature in their cooking liquid. Serve at once or transfer to a shallow baking dish, cover tightly and store 2–3 days in the refrigerator.

Serve the beans chilled, at room temperature, or warmed. Drizzle with olive oil and garnish with parsley and diced tomatoes.

COWBOY BEANS

Basic Barbecue Sauce (page 231) 1 cup (8 fl oz/250 ml)

Thick-cut smoked bacon ½ lb (250 g)

Small onion, 1, diced

Salt and ground pepper

Dried Great Northern or small white (navy) beans ½ lb (250 g), soaked overnight in water to cover and drained

Tomato ketchup ½ cup (4 fl oz/125 ml)

Light brown sugar ¼ cup (2 oz/60 g), firmly packed

Molasses ¼ cup (3 oz/90 g)

Red wine vinegar 2 tablespoons

Dijon mustard 2 tablespoons

Dry mustard 1 tablespoon

Granulated garlic and chile powder 1 tablespoon *each*

Smoke adds a distinctly campfire taste to this frontier classic. Throw in leftover smoked pork, ribs, or brisket for a more substantial dish. Make sure the pot you choose will fit under the cover of your grill, or cook the beans in a fire pit, or over a campfire cowboy style. Serve as a side dish with plenty of grilled bread for mopping up the sauce.

Prepare a **CHARCOAL** or **GAS** grill for **DIRECT** grilling over **MEDIUM** heat (pages 15–16).

In a large, heavy-lidded pot or Dutch oven over medium heat, cook the bacon until crisp and the fat begins to render, 8–10 minutes. Discard the fat, leaving a few tablespoons in the pot. Add the onion to the pot, season with salt and pepper, and cook, stirring, until soft, 5–7 minutes. With a wooden spoon, stir in the beans, barbecue sauce, ketchup, brown sugar, molasses, vinegar, Dijon and dry mustards, granulated garlic, and chile powder. Add enough water to just cover the beans, up to 2 cups (16 fl oz/500 ml), and stir well.

Place the pot on the grill rack over the hottest part of the fire. Or, keep the pot on the burner at medium heat. Partially cover the pot and simmer the beans, stirring occasionally, until deep dark brown in color and thick, 1½–2 hours. Serve at once.

GRILLED FINGERLING POTATOES

There are many varieties of delicious small potatoes available year-round at better supermarkets and farmers' markets. Look for uniform size and smooth skins. Small potatoes need to be parboiled for a short time before grilling to ensure tenderness.

Bring a pot three-fourths full of salted water to a boil. Add the potatoes and return to a boil. Cover, reduce the heat to medium-high, and parboil until they can be pierced with the tip of a knife but are not completely tender, about 10 minutes. Drain. In a large bowl, combine the warm potatoes and the ½ cup (4 fl oz/125 ml) wine and toss to coat. Let cool to room temperature, tossing often. Cut the potatoes in half lengthwise and brush with oil.

In a bowl, stir together the mayonnaise, mustard, the 2 tablespoons white wine, the parsley, and tarragon. Let the dressing stand for 10 minutes.

Prepare a **CHARCOAL** or **GAS** grill for **DIRECT** grilling over **MEDIUM-HIGH** heat (pages 15–16). Brush and oil the grill grate or a vegetable-grilling basket.

Arrange the potatoes on the grill grate or in the basket directly over medium-high heat. Grill, turning once, until grill marks appear, about 5 minutes per side.

Transfer the grilled potatoes to a large bowl, add the dressing, and toss to coat. Taste and adjust the seasoning with salt and pepper. Serve the potatoes at once or cover tightly, refrigerate for about 1 hour, and serve cold.

Fingerling potatoes such as red Russian, Yukon gold, or any thin-skinned new potato 3 lb (1.5 kg)

White wine ½ cup (4 fl oz/ 125 ml) plus 2 tablespoons

Olive oil for brushing

Mayonnaise ½ cup (4 fl oz/125 ml)

Whole-grain mustard 1 tablespoon

Fresh flat-leaf (Italian) parsley 2 tablespoons minced

Fresh tarragon 2 tablespoons minced

Salt and ground pepper

WILD RICE SALAD

MAKES 6–8 SERVINGS

Wild rice is a whole grain, or seed, from an aquatic grass. It is delicious, high in protein and fiber, and is reputed to have nourished American Indians on the Great Plains since the earliest days and contributed to their vitality and strength. Serve this salad as a side dish for grill-roasted turkey and game birds.

Combine the oils in a glass measuring cup. In a medium bowl, whisk the mustard with the wine and vinegar. Add the shallot and 1 teaspoon each salt and pepper. Add the oils in a slow steady stream, whisking constantly. Set vinaigrette aside.

Rinse uncooked wild rice in a sieve and soak in a bowl of water to cover for 30 minutes. Drain well. In a heavy-bottomed saucepan with a lid, bring the stock to a boil. Add 1 teaspoon salt and the wild rice and return to a boil; stir and cover. Reduce heat to low and simmer just until rice kernels begin to puff open, 45–55 minutes. Uncover, fluff with a fork, and gently simmer for 5–10 additional minutes. Drain off any excess liquid and spread the wild rice on a baking sheet to cool. (You will have about 2 cups/16 oz/500 g of cooked wild rice.)

In a large nonaluminum bowl, combine the cooked wild rice, cooked brown rice, vegetables, pecans, and the vinaigrette, 1–2 tablespoons at a time, until ingredients are incorporated and lightly coated. (You may not need to use all the vinaigrette. Save any excess for another use.) Season the salad with salt and pepper. Serve at room temperature or cover, refrigerate for 1–2 hours, and let stand at room temperature for 15 minutes before serving chilled.

Grapeseed oil and olive oil ½ cup (4 fl oz/125 ml), *each*

Dijon mustard 1 tablespoon

Chardonnay wine 3 tablespoons

White wine vinegar 1 tablespoon

Shallot 1 medium, minced

Salt and ground pepper

Wild rice ¾ cup (6 oz/180 g)

Vegetable stock or water 2–3 cups (16–24 fl oz/ 500–750 ml)

Brown or white rice 1 cup (5 oz/155 g), cooked

Onion 1 medium, quartered, grilled, and diced

Red and yellow bell peppers (capsicums) 1 *each*, grilled, cored, seeded, and diced

Pecans ½ cup chopped, toasted in a 300°F (150°C) oven for 15 minutes

208   ON THE SIDE

QUINOA SALAD

Lemon juice 1 tablespoon

Extra-virgin olive oil 3 tablespoons

Maple syrup, 1 teaspoon

Sea salt and ground pepper

Unsalted butter 1 tablespoon

Grapeseed oil 1 tablespoon

Onion 1 small, diced

Shallot 1, minced

Quinoa 1 cup (5 oz/155 g)

Vegetable or chicken stock 2 cups (16 fl oz/500 ml)

Orzo pasta ½ cup (3½ oz/ 105 g), cooked

Golden raisins (sultanas) and dried red currants ¼ cup (1½ oz/45 g) *each*, soaked in water for 30 minutes and drained

Almonds ¼ cup (1 oz/30 g) sliced, toasted in a 300°F (150°C) oven for 15 minutes

Quinoa is an ancient Incan grain that has the highest protein content of all the whole grains. Not only is it rich in nutrients and low in saturated fat, but best of all, it is delicious, with a slightly crunchy texture and a mild, nutty, earthy flavor. Look for quinoa in the grain section of your supermarket.

To make the vinaigrette, in a small bowl, whisk together the lemon juice, olive oil, and maple syrup. Season lightly with salt and pepper, and set aside.

To cook the quinoa, heat the butter and grapeseed oil in a small heavy-bottomed saucepan with a lid over medium heat. As soon as the foam subsides, stir in the onion and shallot, season with salt and pepper, and cover the pot. Sweat the onion and shallots until soft, 5–7 minutes. Off the heat, add the quinoa and enough stock to cover by ½ inch (12 mm). Season with 1 teaspoon salt, return to a boil, cover, and gently simmer until quinoa is tender and slightly puffed open and the stock is absorbed, 15–20 minutes. Drain excess liquid from the pan, if any, and spread the quinoa on a baking sheet to cool.

To assemble the salad, in a large nonaluminum bowl, combine the quinoa, cooked orzo, golden raisins, and red currants. Drizzle with vinaigrette and toss to coat. Taste and adjust the seasoning with salt and pepper. Transfer the quinoa salad to a large bowl, sprinkle toasted almond slices on top, and serve at once.

FARRO SALAD

Vegetable stock or salted water
4 cups (32 fl oz/1 l)

Pearled farro 1½ cups
(9 oz/280 g)

Fresh English peas 1 lb
(500 g), shelled

Extra-virgin olive oil ¼ cup
(2 fl oz/60 ml)

Zest and juice of 1 lemon

Salt and ground pepper

Red and yellow bell peppers
(capsicums) 3, peeled, seeded,
and diced

Red and yellow cherry tomatoes
1 pint (12 oz/375 g), halved

Red onion ¼ cup (1½ oz/45 g)
finely diced

Fresh flat-leaf (Italian)
parsley ½ cup (¾ oz/20 g)
minced

Fresh basil leaves 10, rolled
together and sliced into ribbons

Fresh tarragon, chervil, and
chives 1 tablespoon *each*,
minced

One of the world's oldest grains, farro is a high-protein form of wheat with a nutty, earthy flavor. It is often used as a substitute for barley or rice in soups, and can also be simply dressed with oil and lemon juice and served cold, as in this recipe.

In a large pot, bring the stock to a boil. Add the farro and stir with a large spoon. Return to a boil, reduce the heat to low, partially cover, and cook the farro until al dente, 15–20 minutes. Spread in a shallow pan to cool.

Bring a small saucepan three-fourths full of salted water to a boil. Have ready a bowl of ice water. Boil the peas until tender, about 2 minutes. Drain into a colander. Pour the peas into the ice bath and drain again.

To make a vinaigrette, in a small bowl, whisk together the olive oil and lemon zest and juice. Season to taste with salt and pepper.

In a large salad bowl, combine the farro, peas, bell peppers, tomatoes, onion, parsley, basil, tarragon, chervil, and chives. Add the vinaigrette and toss to coat. Taste and adjust the seasoning with salt and pepper.

Serve at room temperature or cover, refrigerate for 1–2 hours, and let stand at room temperature for 15 minutes before serving.

BLACK BEAN SALAD

This black bean salad is best served when the vegetables are still slightly warm from the grill, or at room temperature within 1 to 2 hours of grilling. The beans and vegetables should be mildly spiced and glistening with the vinaigrette.

To make the vinaigrette, in a small bowl, whisk together the olive oil, lime juice, vinegar, cumin, chile powder, salt, pepper, and a few dashes of hot-pepper sauce.

Prepare a **CHARCOAL** or **GAS** grill for **DIRECT** grilling over **MEDIUM-HIGH** heat (pages 15–16). Brush and oil the grill grate or a vegetable-grilling basket. Brush the onions, bell peppers, and chiles with oil.

Arrange the onions, bell peppers, and chiles on the rack or in the vegetable-grilling basket over the hottest part of the fire. Grill, turning occasionally, until well charred on all sides, about 10 minutes total.

Transfer the grilled vegetables to a bowl, cover, and let steam for 10 minutes. Pick over the vegetables, removing most of the burned skin and leaving some charred bits. Dice the grilled vegetables to a uniform size and place in a large salad bowl.

Add the black beans, cilantro, onion, and vinaigrette and toss to coat evenly. Serve warm or at room temperature.

VINAIGRETTE

Extra-virgin olive oil ¼ cup (2 fl oz/60 ml)

Fresh lime juice 3 tablespoons

Red wine vinegar 2 tablespoons

Cumin and chile powder 1 tablespoon *each*

Salt 1 teaspoon

Ground pepper ½ teaspoon

Hot-pepper sauce

Onions 2 small, quartered

Yellow and red bell peppers (capsicums) 2 *each*, quartered and seeded

Anaheim and jalapeño chiles 2 *each*, halved and seeded

Black beans 2 cans (15 oz/ 470 g each), drained and rinsed

Fresh cilantro (fresh coriander) 1 bunch, leaves only, chopped

Red onion 1 medium, diced

Drinks

Fresh mint 20 leaves, plus 4 mint sprigs for garnish

Simple Syrup 4 fl oz (125 ml) (see below)

White rum 3 fl oz (90 ml)

Fresh lime juice 4 fl oz (125 ml) (from about 4 limes)

Sparkling water 750 ml (24 fl oz)

Blood oranges 2, halved

BLOOD ORANGE MOJITO

The mojito is a classic Cuban cocktail. In this twist on the original, lime and mint are accentuated with blood oranges which are typically in season from late winter through mid-spring. This recipe can be multiplied to make a large batch.

Fill 4 highball glasses with ice. In a glass pitcher, combine the mint leaves and simple syrup. With a muddler or pestle, gently muddle the mint leaves, being careful not to tear them. Stir in the rum and lime juice. Fill the glasses about two-thirds full with the mixture, being sure to get a few mint leaves into each glass. Top the drinks with sparkling water, leaving a little room at the top, and gently stir. Using a reamer, squeeze an orange half over each drink. Garnish each drink with a mint sprig and serve.

Guava nectar 18 fl oz (560 ml)

White rum 9 fl oz (280 ml)

Fresh lime juice 3 fl oz (90 ml) (from about 3 limes)

Simple Syrup 3 fl oz (90 ml) (see note)

Sparkling water 750 ml (24 fl oz)

Lime wedges 6

GUAVA LIME COOLER

Guava is a tropical fruit with a pink flesh and hints of apple and strawberry. Guava nectar is available at both gourmet and Mexican grocery stores. This recipe can be multiplied to make a large batch.

Fill 6 highball glasses with ice. In a pitcher, stir together the guava nectar, rum, lime juice, and simple syrup. Pour into the glasses and top each with a splash of sparkling water. Garnish each drink with a straw and lime wedge and serve.

HOW TO MAKE SIMPLE SYRUP

In a measuring cup, stir together ¼ cup (1¼ oz/37 g) superfine (caster) sugar and ¼ cup (2 fl oz/60 ml) hot water until dissolved. Let cool. This recipe makes 3 fl oz (90 ml) and can be doubled or tripled as needed.

CAIPIRINHA

Cachaça is Brazilian rum made from the juice of freshly squeezed sugar cane, which gives it a vibrant flavor. Muddling the limes extracts oils from their skin. Be careful not to muddle too roughly, as the resulting drink will be bitter.

Limes 2 large

Superfine (caster) sugar ¼ cup (2 oz/60 g)

Cachaça 8 fl oz (250 ml)

Have ready 4 old-fashioned glasses.

Slice off the ends of the limes and cut each lime into 8 wedges. Place 4 wedges in each glass and sprinkle each with 1 tablespoon sugar. With a muddler or pestle, firmly muddle the sugar into the limes until all of the juice has been squeezed. To serve, fill the glasses with ice, top each with 2 fl oz (60 ml) of cachaça, and stir. Serve each drink with a short straw or swizzle stick.

SPARKLING MINT LEMONADE

The ultimate summer quencher, lemonade is refreshing as it is, but can be wonderfully lightened with sparkling water and fresh mint. The result is a nonalcoholic punch similar to a mojito.

MAKES 12 DRINKS

Fresh mint leaves 1 cup (1 oz/ 30 g), plus extra for garnish

Simple Syrup (page 217) 8 fl oz/250 ml

Fresh lemon juice 1 cup (8 fl oz/250 ml; from about 4 large lemons)

Cold water 6 cups (48 fl oz/1.5 l)

Sparkling water 750 ml (24 fl oz)

Lemon wheels for garnish

In a punch bowl, combine the mint leaves and simple syrup. With a muddler or wooden spoon, gently muddle the mint leaves, being careful not to tear them. Stir in the lemon juice and cold water. Add ice and 2 cups (16 fl oz/500 ml) sparkling water. Garnish with lemon wheels and mint leaves.

SUMMER PEACH AGUA FRESCA

MAKES 6 DRINKS

Peaches 4 (2 lb/1 kg), quartered and pitted, plus 6 slices for garnish

Cold water 6 cups (48 fl oz/1.5 l)

Superfine (caster) sugar ¼ cup (2 oz/60 g) or more to taste

Fresh lime juice 1 fl oz (30 ml) (about 1 lime)

Vanilla extract (essence)

Agua fresca, *Spanish for fresh or cold water, is a sweet, juice-like drink that can be made with different fruits. Peaches make a wonderful* agua fresca. *The vanilla accents the flavor, but be careful not to use more than one drop or it can dominate the drink.*

In a blender, combine the peaches, water, ¼ cup sugar, the lime juice, and 1 drop of vanilla and process until smooth. Taste and add more sugar, if desired. Pour through a fine-mesh sieve into a pitcher; discard the pulp. Strain again for added clarity, if desired. Cover and refrigerate until chilled.

To serve, fill 6 old-fashioned glasses with ice. Stir the *agua fresca*, and then pour over the ice. Garnish each drink with a peach slice.

PERFECT ICED TEA

MAKES 6 DRINKS

Oolong tea 5 bags

Orange spice tea 3 bags

Boiling water 20 fl oz (625 ml)

Baking soda (bicarbonate of soda)

Honey 1 tablespoon, plus more to taste

Cold water 4 cups (32 fl oz/1 l)

Lemon wedges for garnish

For this recipe, baking soda helps curb any bitterness and prevents the tea from getting cloudy. Always make iced tea in a glass or ceramic container, never plastic.

Place the tea bags in a pitcher and pour the boiling water over the top. Add a pinch of baking soda, cover, and let steep for 4 minutes. Remove and discard the tea bags; do not squeeze the tea bags. Stir in the honey and cold water. Let cool to room temperature; do not refrigerate while warm. Fill 6 tall glasses with ice and pour the tea over the top. Garnish each drink with a lemon wedge and serve.

LIMONCELLO DIRTY MARTINI

MAKES 4 DRINKS

Lemon twists 4

4 olives

Limoncello 2 fl oz (60 ml)

Vodka 8 fl oz (250 ml)

Extra-dry vermouth 2 fl oz (60 ml)

Olive brine 1 fl oz (30 ml)

Hailing from sunny southern Italy, limoncello is made by infusing a neutral spirit with lemon peel, and then sweetening it with sugar. In Italy it is served in very small glasses as an aperitif or digestif. Paired with vermouth, it makes a delicious savory cocktail.

Wrap each lemon twist around an olive and fasten with a toothpick.

Chill 4 martini glasses in the freezer until frosted. In a glass pitcher, combine the limoncello, vodka, vermouth, and olive brine. Fill the pitcher one-half to three-fourths full with ice and stir until very cold. Strain into the chilled glasses, garnish each drink with a lemon twist–olive, and serve.

FROZEN PASSION FRUIT MARGARITA

MAKES 4 DRINKS

Passion fruit nectar 8 fl oz (250 ml)

Silver tequila 6 fl oz (180 ml)

Fresh lime juice 3 fl oz (90 ml) (from about 3 limes)

Simple Syrup (page 217) 2 fl oz (60 ml)

Ice

Lime wedges 6

Passion fruit is very acidic, so it's not necessary to use as much lime juice in this recipe as in a traditional margarita. If you prefer a margarita on the rocks, blend the drink for a shorter period of time, and then strain it into a glass filled with ice.

Chill 4 rocks glasses in the freezer until frosted. In a blender, combine the passion fruit nectar, tequila, lime juice, simple syrup, and ice. Process on high speed until smooth and slushy. Pour into the chilled glasses, garnish each drink with a lime wedge, and serve.

Ale, such as Bass 3 bottles
(12 fl oz/375 ml each), chilled

Stout, such as Guinness 2 cans
(16 fl oz/500 ml each), chilled

BLACK & TAN

Served in British pubs for more than a century, the Black & Tan is made up of a layering of stout resting on top of a denser ale. The proportion is often 50-50, but a ratio of 9 ounces (280 ml) ale to 7 ounces (220 ml) stout looks and tastes better in a pint glass.

Chill 4 pint glasses in the freezer until frosted. Fill the chilled glasses halfway with the ale. Hold a wide spoon upside down just over the top of the ale, slowly pour the stout over the spoon until the glass is full, and serve.

Fresh lemon juice 2 fl oz (60 ml)
(from about 1 large lemon)

Simple Syrup (page 217) 2 fl oz
(60 ml)

Cold water 1½ cups
(12 fl oz/375 ml)

Gin 4 fl oz (125 ml)

Perfect Iced Tea (page 219)
12 fl oz (375 ml)

Lemon twists 4

SPIKED ARNOLD PALMER

The favorite drink of the champion golfer for whom it is named, this nonalcoholic beverage is nothing more than an equal blend of iced tea and lemonade. Adding a spirit easily converts the Arnold Palmer to a cocktail.

To make the lemonade, in a measuring cup, stir together the lemon juice, simple syrup, and water.

Fill 4 highball glasses with ice. Pour 1 fl oz (30 ml) gin into each glass. Top with 3 oz (90 ml) iced tea and 2 oz (60 ml) lemonade and stir until combined. Garnish each drink with a lemon twist and serve.

Sauces • Marinades • Rubs

Grilled Foods Pairing Chart

Mix and Match Flavor

Good grilling is about good flavoring. Mix up flavors by using the chart below to match different sauces, marinades, rubs, and glazes with whatever you are putting on the grill.

	SAUCES	MARINADES	RUBS	GLAZES
BEEF	Basic Barbecue Sauce, 231 Molasses Barbecue Sauce, 231 Ginger Dipping Sauce, 236 Salsa Verde, 238	Cilantro-Lime Marinade, 238 Tequila-Lime Marinade, 240 Adobo Marinade, 240 Bourbon Marinade, 241	Sicilian Spice Rub, 243 Chile Rub, 245	Mustard Glaze, 246 Soy Glaze, 248
PORK	Basic Barbecue Sauce, 231 Molasses Barbecue Sauce, 231 Portuguese Piri-Piri Sauce, 232 Memphis Mop Sauce, 232	Adobo Marinade, 240 Bourbon Marinade, 241 Dark Beer Marinade, 243	Herbes de Provence Rub, 244 Chile Rub, 245	Mustard Glaze, 246 Spicy Honey Glaze, 246
POULTRY	Basic Barbecue Sauce, 231 Molasses Barbecue Sauce, 231 Portuguese Piri-Piri Sauce, 232	Adobo Marinade, 240 Spicy Marinade, 237 Jerk Marinade, 241 Dark Beer Marinade, 243	Sicilian Spice Rub, 243 Herbes de Provence Rub, 244 Brown Sugar–Herb Rub, 244 Chile Rub, 245	Mustard Glaze, 246 Citrus Glaze, 248 Soy Glaze, 248
FISH	Portuguese Piri-Piri Sauce, 232 Recado Rojo Sauce, 233 Salsa Verde, 238	Cilantro-Lime Marinade, 238 Tequila-Lime Marinade, 240	Sicilian Spice Rub, 243 Herbes de Provence Rub, 244 Horseradish Rub, 245	Citrus Glaze, 248 Soy Glaze, 248
VEGETABLES	Basic Barbecue Sauce, 231 Sweet & Sour Sauce, 233 Salsa Verde, 238	Spicy Marinade, 237 Jerk Marinade, 241	Sicilian Spice Rub, 243 Herbes de Provence Rub, 244 Chile Rub, 245 Horseradish Rub, 245	Citrus Glaze, 248 Soy Glaze, 248

BASIC BARBECUE SAUCE

Serve this sweet and savory barbecue sauce as a condiment for grilled meats and vegetables. This sauce is puréed until smooth but it can also be left a little chunky, if you prefer.

Olive oil 2 tablespoons

Unsalted butter 2 tablespoons

Sweet onion 1 small, diced

Salt and ground pepper

Light brown sugar 2 tablespoons

Chile powder and ground cumin 1 teaspoon *each*

Tomato ketchup 1½ cups (12 fl oz/375 ml)

Prepared barbecue sauce ½ cup (4 oz/125 g)

Molasses 2 tablespoons

Worcestershire sauce 1 tablespoon

In a heavy saucepan over medium heat, warm the oil and melt the butter. Add the diced onions and 2 tablespoons water and season with salt and pepper. Cover and cook, stirring occasionally, until the onions are very soft, 5–7 minutes. Stir in the brown sugar, chile powder, and cumin until the onions are coated. Stir in the ketchup, barbecue sauce, molasses, and Worcestershire sauce. Simmer for 15 minutes. Pour the sauce into a blender and process until smooth. Taste and adjust the seasoning.

Use at once or tightly cover and refrigerate for up to 1 week.

MOLASSES BARBECUE SAUCE

This molasses and bourbon sauce is a good alternative to store-bought sauces that rely heavily on artificial sweeteners and flavorings. Deep and dark, this sauce is a winner with burgers and beef.

Cider vinegar ½ cup (4 fl oz/125 ml)

Molasses ¼ cup (3 oz/90 g)

Bourbon ¼ cup (2 fl oz/60 ml)

Light brown sugar ¼ cup (2 oz/60 g)

Tomato ketchup 2 tablespoons

Dry mustard 1 tablespoon

Granulated garlic, chile powder, dried oregano, allspice, salt, and ground pepper 1 teaspoon *each*

Ground cinnamon ½ teaspoon

Hot-pepper sauce

In a small saucepan over medium heat, combine the vinegar, molasses, bourbon, brown sugar, ketchup, mustard, granulated garlic, chile powder, oregano, allspice, salt, pepper, cinnamon, and hot-pepper sauce to taste. Bring to a boil, whisking to dissolve the sugar. Reduce the heat to medium-low and simmer until the sauce thickens, 15–20 minutes.

Use at once or tightly cover and refrigerate for up to 1 week.

PORTUGUESE PIRI-PIRI SAUCE

When Portuguese sailors returned from colonies in South America and Africa, they brought back with them piri-piri chiles, which became a staple in Portuguese-speaking countries around the world.

In a glass jar, combine the chiles, red pepper paste, vinegar, and salt. Add enough water to just cover the chiles. Tightly cover and shake well. Refrigerate for at least 3 days or up to 3 weeks.

Pour the mixture into a blender and purée. Taste and adjust the seasoning with salt, vinegar, and water; the sauce should be very hot.

Use at once or tightly cover and refrigerate for up to 1 month.

MAKES 2 CUPS (16 FL OZ/500 ML)

Piri-piri, cayenne, or Thai chiles 10–20, about 1½ cups (12 oz/ 375 g), seeded and roughly chopped

Hot red pepper paste, preferably massa de pimentão 3 tablespoons

Distilled white vinegar ¼ cup (2 fl oz/60 ml), plus more as needed

Salt 1½ teaspoons

MEMPHIS MOP SAUCE

In authentic southern-style American barbecue, vinegar-based mop sauces are applied to baste pork in the barbecue pit or on the grill. For added flavor add a splash of hot-pepper sauce.

In a large bowl, whisk together the vinegar, salt, and sugar. Stir in the onion, red pepper flakes, and black pepper. Pour into a tall container.

Use at once or tightly cover and refrigerate for up to 1 week.

MAKES 2 CUPS (16 FL OZ/500 ML)

Cider vinegar 2 cups (16 fl oz/250 ml)

Coarse salt 1 tablespoon

Granulated sugar 1 tablespoon

Small onion 1, thinly sliced

Red pepper flakes 1 tablespoon

Cracked pepper 1 tablespoon

Fresh lime juice ¼ cup
(2 fl oz/60 ml), about 2–3 limes

Tomato ketchup
½ cup (4 fl oz/125 ml)

Soy sauce 1 tablespoon

Light agave syrup 1 tablespoon

Granulated sugar 1 tablespoon

Sweet Thai chile sauce 1
tablespoon, plus more to taste

SWEET & SOUR SAUCE

Sour, salty, and sweet are the best qualities of good sweet and sour sauce. To add a little heat, sweet Thai chile sauce is added, with more at your own discretion. This recipe can be easily doubled.

In a small bowl, whisk the lime juice into the ketchup. Stir in the soy sauce, agave syrup, sugar, and chile sauce. Adjust the seasoning with more lime juice or soy sauce.

Use at once or tightly cover and refrigerate for up to 1 month.

MAKES ¾ CUP (6 OZ/180 G)

Annato seeds and black peppercorns 1 tablespoon *each*

Allspice berries 3

Ground cinnamon ¼ teaspoon

Bottled sour orange juice ¼ cup
(2 fl oz/60 ml)

Garlic 4 cloves, crushed into a paste

Distilled white vinegar 1 teaspoon

RECADO ROJO SAUCE

Sour orange juice can be found in Mexican or Latin American markets. If you are unable to find it, substitute with ¼ cup (2 fl oz/60 ml) fresh orange juice plus 2 tablespoons lime juice.

In a spice grinder or blender, combine the annato seeds, peppercorns, allspice berries, and cinnamon and process into a fine powder. In a nonaluminum bowl, stir together the spice mixture, sour orange juice, garlic paste, and vinegar.

Cover and refrigerate for 30 minutes before using.

ASIAN DIPPING SAUCE

Mirin is a type of rice wine that adds sweetness and flavor to this sauce. It can be found in Asian markets. If you can't find it, substitute with another type of rice wine.

Peel, core, and finely dice the pear. Trim the green onions, including 1 inch (2.5 cm) of the tender green tops, and then thinly slice.

In a nonaluminum bowl, whisk together the pear, green onions, garlic, soy sauce, sherry, mirin, sesame oil, brown sugar, honey, ginger, red pepper flakes, and sesame seeds.

Transfer to a small serving bowl and serve at once.

MAKES 1 CUP (8 FL OZ/250 ML)

Asian pear 1

Green (spring) onions 2

Garlic 2–3 cloves, minced

Soy sauce and dry sherry ½ cup (4 fl oz/125 ml) *each*

Mirin and Asian sesame oil 2 tablespoons *each*

Light brown sugar 1 tablespoon

Honey 1 tablespoon

Fresh ginger 2 teaspoons peeled and grated

Red pepper flakes and toasted sesame seeds 1 teaspoon *each*

GINGER DIPPING SAUCE

The refreshing and slightly sweet taste of ginger pairs well with fish and beef. Use this sauce to accompany skewers of grilled meat or seafood. A red serrano chile may be substituted for the Thai chile.

In a medium bowl, whisk together the soy sauce, mirin, sesame oil, lime juice, and honey. Stir in the ginger, garlic, and chile, if using.

Transfer to a small serving bowl and serve at once.

MAKES 1 CUP (8 FL OZ/250 ML)

Soy sauce ½ cup (4 fl oz/125 ml)

Mirin ¼ cup (2 fl oz/60 ml)

Asian sesame oil 2 tablespoons

Juice of 1 lime

Honey 1–2 tablespoons

Fresh ginger 2 tablespoons, peeled and minced

Garlic 2 cloves, minced

Thai chile 1, finely sliced (optional)

BASIL–GREEN GARLIC DIPPING SAUCE

MAKES 1 CUP (8 FL OZ/250 ML)

Fresh basil leaves ½ cup
(½ oz/15 g)

Olive oil ¼ cup (2 fl oz/60 ml)

Garlic 4 cloves, sliced

Green garlic 2 heads, chopped

Shallot 1, minced

White wine 1–2 tablespoons

Chicken stock ¼ cup
(2 fl oz/60 ml)

Salt and ground pepper

This dipping sauce calls for chicken stock but vegetable stock can also be used. Buy a low-sodium version so you can control the flavor by adding the amount of salt that you desire.

In a medium saucepan over high heat, bring 1 cup (8 fl oz/250 ml) salted water to a boil. Have ready a bowl full of ice and cold water. Add the basil leaves to the boiling water and blanch for 10–20 seconds. Drain, and then plunge into the ice bath. Drain again and pat dry with paper towels. Return the saucepan to the stove top over medium heat. Warm the oil and stir in the garlic and green garlic, shallot, and wine. Cover and cook until soft, 3–5 minutes. Add the basil leaves and cook for 10–20 seconds longer.

Pour the mixture into a blender. Purée, adding the chicken stock to make a smooth, pourable sauce. Taste and adjust the seasoning with salt and pepper. Serve at once.

SPICY MARINADE

MAKES ¾ CUP (6 FL OZ/180 ML)

Fresh ginger 2 tablespoons, peeled and grated

Soy sauce ½ cup (4 fl oz/125 ml)

Fish sauce and sesame oil
2 tablespoons *each*

Garlic 3 cloves, minced

Green (spring) onions 2, thinly sliced

Medium shallot 1, minced

Thai chile 1, seeded and thinly sliced

Zest and juice of 1 lime

This marinade also doubles as a dipping sauce. Serve with grilled poultry or beef to add an Asian flare. Fish sauce and sesame oil can be found in Asian markets or in most well-stocked supermarkets.

In a medium bowl, whisk together the ginger, soy sauce, fish sauce, sesame oil, garlic, green onions, shallot, chile, and lime zest and juice.

Use as a marinade or transfer to a small serving bowl to use as a dipping sauce. Serve at once.

CILANTRO-LIME MARINADE

This marinade adds an exotic accent to anything that goes on the grill. Marinate beef tri-tip or flank steak for up to 1 hour and no more than 5 minutes for fish and shellfish.

Using a microplane grater, remove enough zest from the limes to measure 2 tablespoons; halve and juice the fruits as needed to measure 1 cup (8 fl oz/250 ml) juice. In a blender or food processor, combine the lime zest and juice and the cilantro. Pulse several times, and then scrape down the sides of the bowl with a rubber spatula. Add the oil and pulse a few times until incorporated.

The marinade should be used the day it is made, when it is most flavorful, but can be tightly covered and refrigerated for up to 2 days.

MAKES 2 CUPS (16 FL OZ/500 ML)

Limes 8–10

Fresh cilantro (fresh coriander) 1 bunch, leaves and tender stems only

Vegetable oil such as canola, safflower, or grapeseed ¼ cup (2 fl oz/60 ml)

SALSA VERDE

This delicious green salsa goes equally well with tortilla chips as it does with almost any type of grilled meat. It adds a little heat and a distinct Mexican flavor.

Cut the chiles into quarters and seed them. Leave a few seeds in, if desired, for a spicier salsa. Husk and quarter the tomatillos.

Pick the leaves and tender stems off of the cilantro. Set aside.

In a food processor, combine the chiles, tomatillos, cilantro leaves and stems, parsley, onion, garlic, 1 tablespoon each salt and pepper, and 2 tablespoons lime juice. Pulse several times until combined but still fairly chunky. Stir in the grapeseed oil. Taste and adjust the seasoning with salt, pepper, and lime juice; the salsa should be vibrant green in color. Serve at once or tightly cover and refrigerate for up to 2 days.

MAKES 2 CUPS (16 FL OZ/500 ML)

Jalapeño or serrano chiles 3

Tomatillos 6

Fresh cilantro (fresh coriander) and flat-leaf (Italian) parsley 1 bunch *each*

Small white onion 1, quartered

Garlic 6 cloves

Coarse salt and ground pepper

Fresh lime juice 2 tablespoons, plus more to taste

Grapeseed oil ¼ cup (2 fl oz/ 60 ml)

TEQUILA-LIME MARINADE

Here is a refreshing marinade that is suitable for grilled beef, chicken, fish, and shellfish. Tequila and lime are a great match with fresh cilantro, garlic, and onions.

In a dry frying pan over medium heat, toast the coriander seeds and peppercorns until fragrant, 3–4 minutes. Transfer to a plate and let cool completely. Pour the spices into a spice grinder or blender and process into a coarse powder.

Grate the zest from 1 of the limes. Halve and juice the remaining limes as needed to measure ½ cup (4 fl oz/125 ml) juice.

In a nonaluminum bowl, stir together the lime zest and juice, tequila, oil, sugar, onion, garlic, cilantro, cumin, salt, and toasted spice mixture until the sugar is dissolved. Use at once, or tightly cover and refrigerate for up to 1 day.

MAKES 2 CUPS (16 FL OZ/500 ML)

Coriander seeds and peppercorns 1 tablespoon *each*

Limes 6–8

Tequila ¾ cup (6 fl oz/180 ml)

Canola oil ½ cup (4 fl oz/125 ml)

Granulated sugar ¼ cup (2 oz/60 g)

White onion 1 small, sliced

Garlic 3 cloves, minced

Fresh cilantro (fresh coriander) ¾ cup (1 oz/30 g)

Ground cumin ½ teaspoon

Coarse salt 2 teaspoons

ADOBO MARINADE

This marinade imparts a smoky heat to beef, pork, and chicken for Mexican dishes such as burritos, quesadillas, tostadas, and tacos. Reserve half of the adobo as a spicy condiment for a fajita bar.

Using a vegetable peeler, remove 2 strips of orange zest, each 3 inches (7.5 cm) long and ½ inch (12 mm) wide, from 1 of the oranges. Halve and juice the remaining oranges as needed to measure ¾ cup (6 fl oz/180 ml) juice.

Seed the chipotles or leave a few seeds in, if desired, for a spicier marinade.

In a nonaluminum saucepan over high heat, combine all of the ingredients and bring to a boil. Reduce the heat to medium and simmer until reduced by one-third, about 10 minutes. Let cool in the pan. Remove and discard the orange zest strips. Pour the mixture into a blender and process until smooth. Use at once or tightly cover and refrigerate for up to 2 days.

MAKES 2 CUPS (16 FL OZ/500 ML)

Oranges 2–4

Canned chipotle chiles in adobo sauce 6, plus 2 tablespoons adobo sauce

White wine ½ cup (4 fl oz/125 ml)

Yellow onion ½ cup (2 oz/60 g) chopped

Garlic 6 cloves

Fresh lime juice ¼ cup (2 fl oz/ 60 ml)

Tomato paste 2 tablespoons

Dried oregano 2 teaspoons

Ground cumin, coarse salt, pepper, and chile powder 1 teaspoon *each*

Hot-pepper sauce 2 dashes

BOURBON MARINADE

Bourbon 1 cup (8 fl oz/250 ml)

Light agave syrup ¼ cup
(2 fl oz/60 ml)

Light brown sugar ¼ cup
(2 oz/60 g), lightly packed

Allspice berries 5, or 1 teaspoon
ground allspice

Whole cloves 5

Cracked pepper 1 tablespoon

This marinade gives a subtle sweet bourbon flavor to grilled foods. It is delicious on chicken, turkey, game birds, beef ribs, and pork chops. You can use other types of whiskey in place of the bourbon.

In a small bowl, whisk together the bourbon, agave syrup, and brown sugar until the sugar is dissolved. Stir in the allspice berries, cloves, and pepper.

Use to marinate meat or poultry for at least 1–2 hours or cover tightly and refrigerate for up to 2 days.

JERK MARINADE

MAKES 2 CUPS (16 FL OZ/500 ML)

Scotch bonnet chiles 2–3

Dark rum ¼ cup (2 fl oz/60 ml)

Fresh ginger 2 tablespoons, peeled
and grated

Yellow onion 1, chopped

Shallots 2, quartered

Green onions 1 bunch, chopped

Garlic 2 cloves, roughly chopped

Light brown sugar 3 tablespoons

Soy sauce 4 tablespoons

**Olive oil, lime juice, and malt
vinegar** 3 tablespoons *each*

Fresh thyme leaves 1 tablespoon

Ground allspice 2 teaspoons

Salt and ground pepper

Jerk seasoning comes from the Caribbean island of Jamaica; it is typically a combination of chiles and other spices. Here, it also contains dark rum to give it more island flavor.

Seed and roughly chop the chiles.

In a small saucepan over medium-high heat, bring the rum and 2 tablespoons water to a boil and cook for 2 minutes. Set aside.

In a blender or food processor, combine the ginger, chiles, rum mixture, onion, shallots, green onions, garlic, brown sugar, soy sauce, oil, lime juice, malt vinegar, thyme, allspice, 2 teaspoons salt, 1 teaspoon pepper, and 1 cup (8 fl oz/250 ml) water. Process into a smooth paste, adding more water as needed. Taste and adjust the seasoning with salt and pepper. Cover and refrigerate for 4–5 hours before use.

DARK BEER MARINADE

MAKES 1¼ CUPS (10 OZ/315 G)

Dark beer 6 fl oz (375 ml)

Apple juice concentrate ½ cup
(4 fl oz/125 ml), thawed

Light brown sugar ¼ cup
(2 oz/60 g), firmly packed

Coarse salt and cracked pepper
1 tablespoon *each*

Fresh rosemary 1 tablespoon

Allspice berries 5

Whole cloves 3

*This marinade packs in a deep malt flavor to grilled meats. Use
it on pork, game birds, and poultry. For the best flavor, choose
a top-quality dark beer such as Guinness.*

In a nonaluminum bowl, stir together the beer, apple juice concentrate, brown
sugar, salt, pepper, rosemary, allspice berries, and cloves.

Use to marinate meat for at least 1–2 hours or cover tightly and refrigerate
for up to 2 days.

SICILIAN SPICE RUB

MAKES 1 CUP (8 OZ/250 G)

**Dried rosemary, oregano,
marjoram, thyme, and summer
savory** 2 tablespoons *each*

**Granulated garlic or fresh grated
garlic** 1 tablespoon

Coarse salt 2 tablespoons

Cracked pepper 1 tablespoon

Dried red chile flakes 1 teaspoon

*Italian cooks use dried herbs to season foods prior to grilling. Use
this mixture as an all purpose seasoning rub for poultry, beef, veal,
or lamb for a southern Italian flavor.*

In a small bowl, using your fingers, crumble the rosemary, oregano, marjoram,
thyme, and summer savory. Stir in the granulated garlic, salt, pepper, and chile
flakes until well blended.

Store in a tightly covered jar at room temperature for up to 1 week.

BROWN SUGAR–HERB RUB

This sweet herbaceous rub adds mouthwatering flavor to grilled poultry. The fresh sage and thyme may be substituted with dried sage and thyme, just use half of the amount.

In a small bowl, stir together the salt, pepper, brown sugar, thyme, sage, and granulated garlic until well blended.

Use at once or tightly cover and store for up to 1 week at room temperature.

Coarse salt and cracked pepper
2 tablespoons *each*

Light brown sugar
2 tablespoons, lightly packed

Fresh thyme 1 tablespoon roughly chopped

Fresh sage 1 tablespoon finely chopped

Granulated garlic 1 tablespoon

HERBES DE PROVENCE RUB

This simple dried herb mixture adds a distinctive southern French flavor. Use to season lamb, chicken, and grilled summer vegetables such as squash, zucchini (courgettes), and tomatoes.

In a small bowl, using your fingers, crumble the rosemary, thyme, basil, marjoram, summer savory, oregano, and lavender. Stir in the salt and pepper.

Use at once or tightly cover and store for up to 1 week at room temperature.

Dried rosemary, thyme, basil, marjoram, summer savory, and oregano 2 tablespoons *each*

Fresh or dried lavender 1 teaspoon

Coarse salt and cracked pepper
2 tablespoons *each*

HORSERADISH RUB

MAKES 1 CUP (8 OZ/250 G)

Horseradish root 1 piece, 4–5 inches (10–13 cm) long, peeled

Coarse salt 2 tablespoons

Ground white pepper 1 tablespoon

Granulated sugar 1 tablespoon

Vermouth, vodka, or distilled white vinegar 1–2 tablespoons

Fresh horseradish has a sharp, strong flavor well suited for grilled fish just prior to grilling. Use to season whole fish, fish steaks, or fillets such as salmon, bluefish, mackerel, and sardines.

Using a box grater, finely grate the horseradish to measure ½ cup (5 oz/155 g).

In a small bowl, stir together the horseradish, salt, white pepper, and sugar. Stir in the vermouth to moisten the mixture.

Use at once or tightly cover and store for up to 1 week in the refrigerator.

CHILE RUB

MAKES 1 CUP (8 OZ/250 G)

Coarse salt 3 tablespoons

Light brown sugar 2 tablespoons, firmly packed

Paprika 1½ tablespoons

Cracked pepper and granulated garlic 1 tablespoon *each*

Dry mustard, cumin, chile powder, and dried oregano 1 teaspoon *each*

This is an all-purpose spice rub for slow and low barbecue cooking. It is best used liberally to coat beef, poultry, and pork overnight. It can also be rubbed onto the meat just before it is placed on the grill.

In a spice grinder or blender, combine the salt, brown sugar, paprika, pepper, granulated garlic, mustard, cumin, chile powder, and oregano. Process into a coarse powder.

Use at once or tightly cover and store for up to 1 week at room temperature.

SPICY HONEY GLAZE

One of the simplest of all glazes is a combination of honey, agave syrup, and balsamic vinegar. This variation gets an added boost from hot chile powder and ground black pepper.

In a small bowl, stir together the honey, agave syrup, and balsamic vinegar. Add the cayenne, chile powder, and pepper. Mix well.

Brush onto chicken wings, quail, or shrimp on the grill or cover tightly and store in the refrigerator for up to 1 week.

MAKES 1 CUP (8 OZ/250 G)

Honey ¼ cup (3 fl oz/80 ml)

Light agave syrup 2 tablespoons

Balsamic vinegar 2 tablespoons

Cayenne pepper 1 teaspoon

Chile powder 1 teaspoon

Ground pepper 1 teaspoon

MUSTARD GLAZE

Dijon mustard can be livened up with fresh thyme and vermouth for an unbeatable glaze for chicken wings. Brush this glaze on lamb or pork chops and pork tenderloins for a simple and spicy grilled crust.

In a nonaluminum bowl, stir together the Dijon and dry mustards and the thyme.

Stir in the vermouth as needed until the mixture is spreadable. Taste and adjust the seasoning with salt and white pepper; the glaze should be strong tasting, highly spiced, and deep amber in color.

Use at once or tightly cover and store in the refrigerator for up to 1 week.

MAKES 1 CUP (8 OZ/250 G)

Dijon mustard ½ cup (4 oz/125 g)

Dry mustard 1 tablespoon

Fresh thyme 1 teaspoon or ½ teaspoon dried thyme

Dry vermouth 2–3 tablespoons

Coarse salt and ground white pepper

CITRUS GLAZE

Brush this citrus glaze onto chicken wings, chicken satays, shellfish, and summer vegetables on the grill. If you are feeling experimental, use another type of citrus juice such as blood orange.

Using a microplane grater, grate the zest from the lime; halve and juice the fruit.

In a small saucepan over high heat, combine the lime juice, orange juice concentrate, and wine and bring to a boil. Reduce the heat to medium and add the lime zest, agave syrup, and salt. Simmer, whisking to dissolve the syrup, until thick enough to coat the back of a spoon, about 10 minutes. Stir in more wine, 1 tablespoon at a time, if needed to thin the glaze.

Use at once or cover tightly and store in the refrigerator for up to 1 week.

MAKES 1 CUP (8 FL OZ/250 ML)

Lime or lemon 1

Orange juice concentrate ½ cup (4 fl oz/125 ml), thawed, or 1 cup (8 fl oz/250 ml) fresh orange juice, simmered until reduced by one-half

Dry white wine ¼ cup (2 fl oz/ 60 ml), plus wine as needed

Light agave syrup ¼ cup (2 fl oz/60 ml)

Coarse salt ½ teaspoon

SOY GLAZE

Perhaps the simplest of all grilling glazes, comprised of just two pantry ingredients, this flavorful glaze produces a mahogany-colored finish for turkey, chicken, duck, and all game birds.

In a small bowl, whisk together the soy sauce and honey.

Brush onto poultry during the last few minutes of cooking for a mahogany-colored glaze or cover tightly and store in the refrigerator for up to 1 week.

MAKES 1 CUP (10 FL OZ/310 ML)

Soy sauce ½ cup (4 fl oz/125 ml)

Honey or light agave syrup ½ cup (6 fl oz/185 ml)

APPLE-BOURBON BRINE

Brine not only adds flavor, it also enhances the juiciness in your grilled food. Use this recipe as an overnight brine for turkey, chicken, and game birds prior to grilling, spit-roasting, or smoking.

MAKES 2 QT (64 FL OZ/2 L)

Apple cider 4 cups (32 fl oz/1 l)

Bourbon or other whiskey 2 cups (16 fl oz/500 ml)

Coarse salt ½ cup (4 oz/125 g)

Granulated sugar ½ cup (4 oz/125 g)

Yellow onion 1, quartered

Whole bay leaves 3–4

In a clean 5-gallon (20-l) plastic bucket, combine the apple cider and bourbon. Whisk in the salt and sugar until dissolved. Add the onion and bay leaves.

Pour over turkey, chicken, or game birds in a large container, stock pot, or clean plastic bucket. Add enough water to cover and weigh down with a plate to submerge the bird in the brine.

SEASONING MIX

This dry mix is a combination of spices and herbs to add flavor to grilled foods. Massage it onto firm, white-fleshed fish or on beef before throwing them on the grill.

MAKES ¾ CUP (6 OZ/185 G)

Sea salt 3 tablespoons

Ground white pepper 1 tablespoon

Paprika 1 tablespoon

Granulated garlic 1 tablespoon

Fresh thyme 1 tablespoon chopped

Red pepper flakes 1 teaspoon

In a small bowl, combine the salt, white pepper, paprika, granulated garlic, thyme, and red pepper flakes.

Use at once or cover tightly and store in the refrigerator for up to 1 week.

Condiments

SPICE-HERB BUTTER

This compound butter is used to flavor grilled turkey but it can be used for other recipes that call for butter. It is also delicious spread on top of grilled bread.

In a spice grinder or blender, combine the peppercorns, fennel, and coriander seeds. Process into a coarse powder. In a small bowl, stir together the spice powder, chopped herbs, butter, granulated garlic, lemon zest and juice, and 1 teaspoon salt.

This butter will keep 1 week in the refrigerator or 3 months in the freezer.

MAKES 1 CUP (8 OZ/250 G)

White peppercorns, fennel seeds, and coriander seeds 2 tablespoons *each*, toasted

Fresh rosemary, sage, and thyme 1 tablespoon *each*, chopped

Unsalted butter 1 cup (8 oz/250 g), at room temperature

Granulated garlic 1 tablespoon

Zest and juice of 1 lemon

Coarse salt

ROSEMARY-THYME BUTTER

Fresh rosemary and thyme need to be crushed and cooked to release their full flavor. A small disc of this butter adds tons of flavor and moisture as it melts on beef, chicken, pork, and fish.

In a small saucepan over medium heat, melt 1 tablespoon butter. Add the rosemary, thyme, and shallot. Cook until fragrant, stirring constantly, 1–2 minutes. Add the wine and reduce until the liquid is almost evaporated, 1–2 minutes longer. Remove from the heat and let cool.

Cream the remaining butter in the bowl of a stand mixer fitted with a paddle attachment on medium speed until butter reaches a creamy consistency. Fold in the herb-shallot mixture. Spread into a log shape on a piece of parchment (baking) paper, fold the bottom over the top, and use a ruler to form a tight cylinder. This butter will keep 1 week in the refrigerator or 3 months in the freezer.

MAKES ¼ LB (4 OZ/125 G)

Unsalted butter ¼ pound (8 tablespoons), at room temperature

Fresh rosemary leaves 2 tablespoons minced

Fresh thyme leaves 2 tablespoons minced

Shallot 1 tablespoon minced

White wine 2 tablespoons

LEMON-TARRAGON BUTTER

MAKES 2 CUPS (1 LB/500 G)

Unsalted butter ¼ lb
(8 tablespoons), at room
temperature

Zest and juice of 1 lemon

Fresh tarragon leaves
2-3 tablespoons minced

Salt and ground white pepper

Lemon and fresh tarragon are a classic French pairing going back over a century. With bright citrus and anise flavors, this butter enhances grilled meats, fish, and shellfish.

Cream the butter in the bowl of a stand mixer fitted with the paddle attachment until it reaches a mayonnaise-like consistency. Drop by drop, add 1–2 tablespoons lemon juice. Beat in the tarragon leaves and season with salt and white pepper.

Spread into a log shape on a piece of parchment (baking) paper, fold the bottom over the top, and use a ruler to form a tight cylinder. Alternatively, pipe the lemon-tarragon butter through a pastry bag fitted with a star tip into floret shapes on a parchment paper-lined baking sheet and chill in the refrigerator to set. This butter will keep 1 week in the refrigerator or 3 months in the freezer.

WASABI BUTTER

MAKES ¼ LB (4 OZ/125 G)

Unsalted butter ¼ pound
(8 tablespoons), at room
temperature

Pure wasabi powder 2 tablespoons

Dijon mustard 1 tablespoon

Fresh grated ginger 2 tablespoons,
squeezed to extract 1–2 teaspoons
ginger juice

Salt and ground pepper

This compound butter, flavored with Japan's green mustard powder, will enrich any daily catch of prized sport fish such as bluefish, striper, swordfish, salmon, tuna, or marlin.

Cream the butter in the bowl of a stand mixer fitted with the paddle attachment until it reaches a creamy consistency. In a small bowl, stir together the wasabi powder, mustard, and ginger juice to form a paste. Beat in the wasabi-mustard paste to the butter and season with salt and pepper.

Spread into a log shape on a piece of parchment (baking) paper, fold the bottom over the top, and use a ruler to form a tight cylinder. This butter will keep 1 week in the refrigerator or 3 months in the freezer.

CHIPOTLE KETCHUP

Add a little kick to your ketchup with a few spices and some chile peppers. For a smoother sauce, purée the mixture in a blender or food processor.

Seed and chop all of the chiles.

In a small saucepan over medium heat, warm the oil. Add the chipotle and jalapeño chiles, onion, and garlic. Cook, stirring occasionally, until soft, 4–5 minutes. Reduce the heat to low and stir in the ketchup, sugar, cumin, and chile powder. Simmer until deep red in color, about 15 minutes. Let cool.

Use at once or tightly cover and refrigerate for up to 1 month.

MAKES 1½ CUPS (12 FL OZ/375 ML)

Canned chipotle chiles in adobo sauce 4

Jalapeño or serrano chile 1

Olive oil 1 tablespoon

Small yellow onion 1, diced

Garlic 2 cloves, minced

Tomato ketchup 1 cup (8 fl oz/250 ml)

Granulated sugar 1 tablespoon

Cumin and chile powder 1 teaspoon *each*

CUCUMBER RELISH

Here is a cooling cucumber salad that matches well with the heat of spicy rubs and fiery sauces prevalent in grilling or barbecue cookery. Use this cucumber relish as a condiment for beef or chicken.

Peel, seed, and cut the cucumber into ¼-inch (6-mm) slices.

In a medium bowl, combine the cucumber, shallot, red onion, vinegar, and sugar. Toss several times to coat and until the sugar dissolves completely. Sprinkle mint on top and toss to coat. Refrigerate to let the flavors meld, 1–2 hours. Just before serving, strain the cucumber relish through a fine mesh sieve, as the cucumber will release up to 1 cup (8 fl oz/250 ml) of liquid. Discard the liquid. Add the salt and pepper and stir to combine.

Use at once or tightly cover and refrigerate for up to 1 week.

MAKES 2 CUPS (1 LB/500 G)

Seedless English (hothouse) cucumber 1

Shallot 1 medium, very finely sliced, rings separated

Red onion ½, finely sliced

Cider vinegar ¼ cup (2 fl oz/60 ml)

Granulated sugar 1 tablespoon

Fresh mint leaves 6–8, minced

Salt and ground pepper 1 teaspoon *each*

MEYER LEMON AIOLI

The Meyer lemon is believed to be a cross between a lemon and an orange and yields a sweeter juice than regular lemons produce. Look for them during the winter and spring months.

Pour the oils into a measuring cup with a spout. In a blender or food processor, combine the egg yolks, mustard, garlic, salt, and white pepper. Pulse several times until the garlic is pulverized. With the motor running, slowly add the oils in a steady stream. Stir in 3 tablespoons of the lemon juice. Stir in the remaining 1 tablespoon lemon juice if needed to thin the aioli; it should be the consistency of mayonnaise. Spoon into a serving bowl, cover, and refrigerate.

MAKES 2 CUPS (1 LB/500 G)

Canola oil and olive oil ¼ cup (2 fl oz/60 ml) *each*

Large egg yolks 3

Dijon mustard 1 tablespoon

Garlic 3 cloves

Salt ½ teaspoon

Ground white pepper ¼ teaspoon

Fresh Meyer lemon juice 3–4 tablespoons

PEPPER AIOLI

This red-hued aioli will add a little heat to your condiment repertoire. Control the heat level by adding just enough hot pepper sauce to suit your liking. Refrigerate until ready to use.

Place the garlic cloves in a small bowl. Add boiling salted water to cover and let stand for 1 minute. Strain the garlic and pat dry; reserve ¼ cup (2 fl oz/60 ml) of the blanching liquid.

In a blender, combine the garlic, egg yolks, red pepper, paprika, chile powder, 1 teaspoon salt, ½ teaspoon pepper, and a few dashes of hot-pepper sauce. Blend until the garlic and red pepper are pulverized. With the motor running, add the oils in a slow steady steam. Stir in the reserved garlic blanching liquid, 1 tablespoon at a time, as needed, to thin the aioli; it should be the consistency of mayonnaise. Taste and adjust the seasoning.

MAKES 2 CUPS (1 LB/500 G)

Garlic 6 cloves

Large egg yolks 2

Red bell pepper (capsicum) 1, grilled, peeled, seeded, and quartered

Sweet paprika and chile powder 1 teaspoon *each*

Salt and ground pepper

Hot-pepper sauce

Olive oil ½ cup (4 fl oz/125 ml)

Canola oil ¼ cup (2 fl oz/60 ml)

MAKES 2 CUPS (1 LB/500 G)

Canola oil ½ cup (4 fl oz/125 ml)

Olive oil ¼ cup (2 fl oz/60 ml)

Large egg yolks 2

Dijon mustard 1 tablespoon

Garlic 3 cloves

Saffron threads ¼ teaspoon, finely chopped

Salt ½ teaspoon

Ground white pepper ¼ teaspoon

Fresh lemon juice 1–2 tablespoons

SAFFRON AIOLI

Saffron is a pungent and earthy spice that goes a long way in small amounts. Look for it in the spice aisle of your market and don't be tempted to buy the powdered form, which loses flavor rapidly.

Combine the oils in a measuring cup with a spout. In a blender or food processor, combine the egg yolks, mustard, garlic, saffron, salt, and white pepper. Pulse several times until the garlic is pulverized. With the motor running, add the oils in a slow steady stream. Stir in 1 tablespoon of the lemon juice. Stir in the remaining 1 tablespoon lemon juice if needed to thin the aioli; it should be the consistency of mayonnaise. Spoon into a serving bowl or individual ramekins, cover, and refrigerate.

MAKES 2 CUPS (1 LB/500 G)

Heavy (double) cream 1 cup (8 fl oz/250 ml)

Crème fraîche ½ cup (4 fl oz/125 ml)

Fresh horseradish ½ cup (4 oz/ 125 g), peeled, grated, and patted dry

Fresh lemon juice 3 tablespoons

Granulated sugar 1 teaspoon

Fresh dill 6–7 fronds, finely chopped

HORSERADISH CRÈME FRAÎCHE

Crème fraîche can be purchased or you can make your own by stirring 1 tablespoon of buttermilk into ½ cup (4 fl oz/125 ml) heavy (double) cream. Cover and set in a warm spot for 24 hours.

In a large bowl, using an electric mixer, whip the cream until soft peaks form, about 5 minutes. Place in the refrigerator.

In a small bowl, using a whisk, whip the crème fraîche until thickened. (It may appear watery at first but will come together to form stiff peaks.) Fold in the horseradish, lemon juice, sugar, and dill.

Fold the crème fraîche mixture into the whipped cream.

Serve at once or tightly cover and refrigerate for up to 4 days.

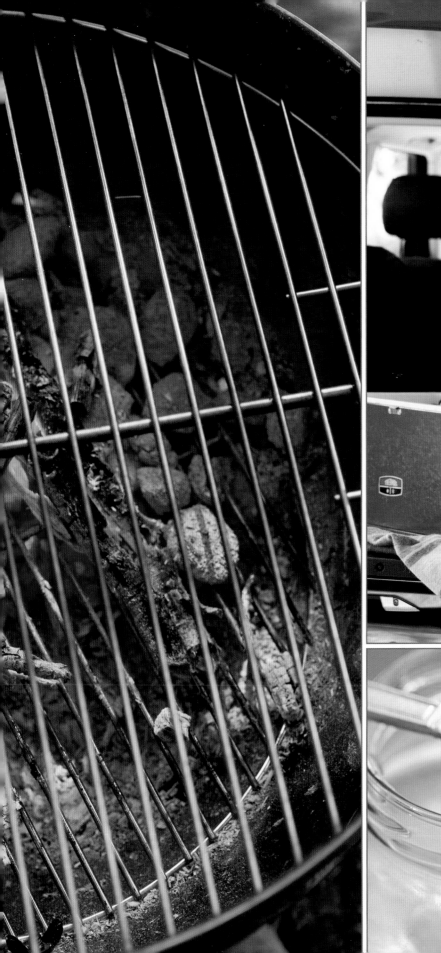

CHAMPAGNE VINAIGRETTE

Champagne vinegar, a vinegar made from Champagne grapes, is the key ingredient here. It has a more subtle, mellow flavor than most other vinegars, making it perfect for salads.

In a medium bowl, combine the grapeseed and olive oils in a measuring cup with a spout. In a nonaluminum bowl, whisk together the vinegar, mustard, shallot, salt, and white pepper. Add the oils in a slow steady stream, whisking constantly. Pour the vinaigrette into a sauceboat or small serving bowl.

Use at once or cover tightly and store in the refrigerator for up to 2 days.

MAKES 1 CUP (8 FL OZ/250 ML)

Grapeseed oil ½ cup (4 fl oz/125 ml)

Extra-virgin olive oil ¼ cup (2 fl oz/60 ml)

Champagne vinegar 2 tablespoons

Dijon mustard 2 tablespoons

Shallot 1, minced

Salt 1 teaspoon

Ground white pepper ½ teaspoon

BUTTERMILK DRESSING

Pack up this refreshing dressing in a glass container, put it on ice, and bring it along to your next picnic to drizzle on salads or vegetables, or toss it on coleslaw.

In a medium bowl, stir together the mayonnaise, buttermilk, and sour cream. Stir in the chopped parsley and chives. Season with salt and white pepper.

Use at once or cover tightly and store in the refrigerator for up to 2 days.

MAKES 1½ CUPS (12 FL OZ/375 ML)

Mayonnaise ¾ cup (6 fl oz/180 ml)

Buttermilk ½ cup (4 fl oz/125 ml)

Sour cream ¼ cup (2 oz/60 g)

Fresh flat-leaf (Italian) parsley ½ bunch, leaves and tender stems, finely chopped

Fresh chives ½ bunch, finely chopped

Salt and ground white pepper

Fresh basil leaves 5–6

Grapeseed oil ½ cup
(4 fl oz/125 ml)

Extra-virgin olive oil ¼ cup
(2 fl oz/60 ml)

Sun-dried tomatoes 2, minced

**Balsamic vinegar and red wine
vinegar** 1 tablespoon *each*

Maple syrup 1 tablespoon

Dijon mustard 1 tablespoon

Salt and ground pepper

TOMATO-BASIL VINAIGRETTE

*Tomato and basil are perfect together and when combined with
a good-quality olive oil, they make a tasty vinaigrette. Serve with
grilled vegetables or on a bed of mixed greens.*

Roll the basil leaves together lengthwise and slice crosswise into thin ribbons.

In a medium bowl, combine the grapeseed and olive oils in a measuring cup with
a spout. In a blender or food processor, combine the sun-dried tomatoes, balsamic
and red wine vinegars, maple syrup, and mustard. Pulse several times to chop the
sun-dried tomatoes and incorporate ingredients into a thick, red paste. With the
motor running, add the oils in a slow steady stream. Add the basil and salt and
pepper to taste; pulse once to incorporate. Pour the vinaigrette into a small bowl.
Use at once or cover tightly and store in the refrigerator for up to 2 days.

Grapeseed oil ¼ cup
(2 fl oz/60 ml)

**Extra-virgin olive oil, balsamic
vinegar, and red wine vinegar**
1 tablespoon *each*

Dijon mustard 1 tablespoon

Garlic 1 clove, minced

Sea salt ½ teaspoon

Ground pepper ¼ teaspoon

BALSAMIC VINAIGRETTE

*This tart vinaigrette is ideal for salads and can also be used as a
dipping sauce for grilled bread. Top-quality olive oil and balsamic
vinegar will yield a better flavor.*

In a bowl, combine the grapeseed and olive oils in a measuring cup with a spout. In
a nonaluminum bowl, whisk together the balsamic and red wine vinegars, mustard,
garlic, salt, and pepper. Add the oils in a slow steady stream, whisking constantly.

Use at once or cover tightly and store in the refrigerator for up to 2 days.

BEER MUSTARD

MAKES ABOUT ¾ CUP (12 OZ/375 G)

Dry mustard ½ cup (1½ oz/45 g)

Amber or dark beer ½ cup (4 fl oz/125 ml)

Cider vinegar 2 tablespoons

Salt ½ teaspoon

Granulated sugar ¼ cup (2 oz/60 g)

Mustard seeds 1 tablespoon, toasted

Large egg 1, beaten

Mustard has always been a favorite among the condiments. Add beer, and it's even better. The darker the beer that you use, the more intense the flavor will be.

Whisk together the mustard, beer, vinegar, and salt in a nonaluminum bowl until smooth. Cover and let stand for at least 2 hours, or overnight.

Transfer to a nonaluminum saucepan. Whisk in the sugar, toasted mustard seeds, and egg, whisking constantly until the mixture reaches a full boil. The mustard should be amber-yellow and strong. Let cool.

Use at once or cover tightly and store in the refrigerator for up to 1 month.

TAPENADE RELISH

MAKES 2 CUPS (1 LB/500 G)

Kalamata or Gaeta olives 2 cups (8 oz/250 g) pitted, or oil-cured olives

Anchovy fillets 3, oil-packed

Crushed red chile flakes 1 teaspoon

Red onion ½, sliced thin

Sea salt, preferably fleur de sel

Ground pepper

Olive tapenade brings a terrific Mediterranean flavor to many grilled foods, from grilled bread, salads, and beef to potatoes, fish, and chicken.

Roughly chop the olives and anchovy fillets.

In a medium bowl, stir together the olives, anchovies, chile flakes, and onion. Season to taste with salt and pepper.

Use at once or cover tightly and refrigerate for up to 1 week.

RHUBARB CHUTNEY

Rhubarb is an intensely tart vegetable that is usually cooked with sugar to mellow the flavor. Here it is used to make a vibrant red chutney that is delicious on grilled chicken or turkey.

In a heavy saucepan over medium-high heat, combine the rhubarb, onion, vinegar, red wine, and ½ cup (4 fl oz/125 ml) water and bring to a boil. Simmer until the rhubarb and onions are soft and the liquid is almost evaporated, about 10 minutes. Stir in the agave syrup, brown sugar, mace, allspice, five-spice powder, garam masala, and cloves. Cook over medium-high heat until the mixture is thick and the liquid is almost evaporated, 5–10 minutes longer. Taste and adjust the seasoning; the chutney should be highly spiced with the consistency of mayonnaise. Spoon into a bowl, cover tightly, and refrigerate for at least 1 hour or up to 4 hours.

MAKES 2 CUPS (1 LB/500 G)

Rhubarb 2 stalks, diced, about 1½ cup (6 oz/180 g) total

Red onion 1, diced

Dry red wine vinegar ¼ cup (2 fl oz/60 ml)

Red wine 3 tablespoons

Light agave syrup 3 tablespoons

Light brown sugar 2 tablespoons

Ground mace, allspice, five-spice powder, and garam masala ½ teaspoon *each*

Ground cloves ¼ teaspoon

CRANBERRY CHUTNEY

If you happen to be making this chutney when fresh cranberries are available, substitute them for frozen. Use this chutney alongside your grilled Thanksgiving turkey.

In a heavy saucepan over medium-high heat, combine the cranberries, pears, onion, ginger, orange juice and zest, vinegar, white wine, and ½ cup (4 fl oz/125 ml) water and bring to a boil. Simmer until the pears and onions are soft and the cranberries begin to pop, 8–10 minutes. Stir in the brown sugar and cinnamon until the sugar is dissolved. Cook over medium-high heat until the liquid is reduced by one-half, about 10 minutes longer. Pour one-third of the mixture into a blender or food processor and process until puréed. Stir the purée into the saucepan. Taste and adjust the seasoning. Cover tightly, and refrigerate for at least 1 hour or up to 4 hours.

MAKES 2 CUPS (1 LB/500 G)

Frozen cranberries ¼ lb (10 oz/315 g), at room temperature

Red pears 2 peeled, cored, and finely diced

Small onion 1, finely diced

Ginger 1 teaspoon peeled and finely grated

Orange juice ¾ cup (6 fl oz/180

Orange zest 1 teaspoon

Apple cider vinegar and white wine ¼ cup (2 fl oz/60 ml) *each*

Light brown sugar ¼ cup (6 oz/185 g)

Ground cinnamon ½ teaspoon

STONE FRUIT CHUTNEY

MAKES 2 CUPS (1 LB/500 G)

Yellow peaches 2 lb (1 kg)

Mango 1, peeled

Fresh or canned pineapple
½ cup (6 oz/185 g), diced

Light agave syrup 3 tablespoons

Cider vinegar 2 tablespoons

Light brown sugar 2 tablespoons,
lightly packed

Ground cinnamon and cardamon
½ teaspoon *each*

Hot-pepper sauce

Fresh cilantro (fresh coriander)
2 tablespoons minced

There is nothing better than summertime and the start of the stone fruit season. In this recipe, the peaches can be replaced with nectarines or you can use a mixture of both.

Pit the peaches and mango and cut each into ½-inch (12-mm) dice.

In a heavy saucepan over medium-high heat, combine the peaches, mango, pineapple, agave syrup, vinegar, brown sugar, cinnamon, cardamom and a few dashes of hot-pepper sauce and bring to a boil. Reduce the heat to medium and cook the chutney, stirring well, until syrupy and thick and the fruit softens, 5–6 minutes. Let cool to room temperature. Stir in the cilantro and serve at once or cover tightly and refrigerate for up to 1 week.

CARAMELIZED ONION JAM

MAKES 2 CUPS (1 LB/500 G)

Red onion 1 medium, peeled,
thinly sliced, about 2 cups

Red wine vinegar ¼ cup (2 fl oz/
60 ml)

Red wine ¼ cup (2 fl oz/60 ml)

Granulated sugar ½ cup (4 oz/
125 g)

Fresh thyme leaves 1 tablespoon

Light agave syrup ¼ cup
(3 fl oz/90 ml)

This caramelized onion jam can be made on the stove top or on a side burner of a gas grill. It is the perfect accompaniment on top of a big, juicy steak or with any type of burger.

In a medium saucepan over medium-high heat, combine the onion, vinegar, red wine, sugar, and thyme and bring to a boil. Reduce the heat to medium-low and cook, stirring occasionally, until the onions are very soft and translucent, about 10 minutes. Add the agave syrup and stir to coat onions. Cook without burning, until the onions begin to caramelize and the mixture is thick and syrupy, 1–2 minutes more. The jam will thicken as it cools.

Serve at once or cover tightly and refrigerate for up to 1 week.

Basic Recipes

Included here are basic recipes that pair well with grilled pork chops, lamb kebabs, chicken, and turkey. Serve them with these suggested dishes or alongside the grilled food of your choice.

GRILLED APPLE PURÉE

Unsalted butter 4 tablespoons (4 oz/125 g)

Light brown sugar 1 cup (7 oz/220 g), firmly packed

Ground cinnamon ½ teaspoon

Ground nutmeg ¼ teaspoon

Ground allspice ¼ teaspoon

Ground cardamom ¼ teaspoon

Ground cloves ¼ teaspoon

Tart white-fleshed apples such as granny smith, gala, or gravenstein 4–6, about 2 lb (1 kg) total weight, peeled, cored, and quartered

Calvados or other brandy 2 tablespoons

MAKES 4 SERVINGS

In a large saucepan over medium-high heat, melt the butter until the foam subsides. Stir in the sugar, cinnamon, nutmeg, allspice, cardamom, and cloves. Reduce the heat to medium-low and stir until the mixture is fragrant and the sugar has melted, 5–7 minutes. Add the apples and Calvados and toss to coat.

On a charcoal or gas grill prepared for direct grilling over medium-high heat, arrange the apples on the grill grate or in a vegetable-grilling basket over the hottest part of the fire. Grill, turning often, until caramelized and soft, 10–12 minutes. Let cool and transfer to the bowl of a food processor.

Meanwhile, working in batches, process the apples until smooth. Taste and adjust the seasoning; the apple purée should be highly spiced. Transfer to a saucepan and keep warm on the grill or stove top or let cool to room temperature.

Grilled Apples with Ice Cream: Grilled apples are delicious when served alongside ice cream. Follow the directions above but omit the puréeing step. Let the grilled apples cool and serve on top of a scoop of vanilla ice cream.

HERBED COUSCOUS

Couscous 2 cups (12 oz/375 g)

Salt

Fresh flat-leaf (Italian) parsley ¼ cup (⅓ oz/10 g) roughly chopped

Fresh tarragon and preserved lemons 2 tablespoons *each,* finely chopped

Sliced almonds 2 tablespoons, toasted

Ground cumin 1 teaspoon

MAKES 6 SERVINGS

In a medium saucepan, over medium heat, add 1½ cups (12 fl oz/375 ml) water and ½ teaspoon salt. When the water boils, remove from the heat and stir in the couscous. Cover and let stand for 10 minutes. In a large bowl, combine the remaining ingredients and toss gently. Serve warm.

MINT RAITA

Whole-milk Greek-style yogurt 2 cups (16 oz/500 g)

Fresh mint 3 tablespoons finely chopped

Fresh cilantro (fresh coriander) 2 tablespoons leaves and stems

Ground cumin ½ teaspoon

Zest and juice of 1 lime

Coarse salt and Garam masala ½ teaspoon *each*

MAKES 6–8 SERVINGS

Place the yogurt in a damp cheesecloth–lined sieve over a bowl. Cover and let drain for at least 1 hour or up to 4 hours; discard the liquid. In a nonaluminum bowl, stir together the yogurt, mint, cilantro, cumin, lime zest, and salt. Add the lime juice, 1 tablespoon at a time, until the sauce is creamy. Taste and adjust the seasoning with lime juice and salt. Pour into a serving bowl and sprinkle with the garam masala. Cover tightly and refrigerate for 1 hour.

COUNTRY-STYLE GRAVY

White wine ½ cup (4 fl oz/125 ml)

Water, chicken stock, or broth ½ cup (4 fl oz/125 ml)

Unsalted butter 2 tablespoons

All-purpose (plain) flour 2 tablespoons

Coarse salt and ground white pepper

MAKES 4 SERVINGS

If using the Grilled Turkey recipe on page 157, mash the roasted vegetables and herb sprigs that are under the turkey in the roasting pan. Return the pan to a grill over direct heat or stove top on medium-high heat and deglaze the bottom of the pan with the white wine and water, using a wooden spoon to dislodge any brown bits. Strain through a sieve into a measuring cup with a spout or beaker; discard the solids. Using a small ladle, skim the grease off the top, leaving 1–2 tablespoons in the cup with the pan juices.

In a saucepan over medium heat, melt the butter until the foam subsides. Stir in the flour, season with salt and white pepper, and cook, stirring constantly, until golden brown, about 2 minutes. Add the strained pan juices, ½ cup (4 fl oz/125 ml) at a time, and briefly remove the pan from the heat, whisking vigorously, after each addition. Simmer the gravy until it is very smooth and thick enough to coat the back of a spoon, about 10 minutes. Taste and adjust the seasoning.

Note: If not using the Grilled Turkey recipe on page 157, roast the following vegetables for the gravy: 3 large carrots, peeled and halved lengthwise; 4 celery ribs; and 2 yellow onions, peeled and quartered.

Index